Love

as Jesus Loved

with Leader's Guide and DVD

BOOK 3 EXPERIENCE THE LIFE

Love
as Jesus Loved
with Leader's Guide and DVD

Transformed Relationships

BILL HULL & PAUL MASCARELLA

NAVPRESS
Discipleship Inside Out™

Discipleship Inside Out™

NavPress is the publishing ministry of The Navigators, an international Christian organization and leader in personal spiritual development. NavPress is committed to helping people grow spiritually and enjoy lives of meaning and hope through personal and group resources that are biblically rooted, culturally relevant, and highly practical.

**For a free catalog go to www.NavPress.com
or call 1.800.366.7788 in the United States or 1.800.839.4769 in Canada.**

ISBN-13: 978-1-61521-557-7

Cover design by Arvid Wallen
Cover image by Shutterstock

Printed in the United States of America

1 2 3 4 5 6 7 8 / 14 13 12 11 10

CONTENTS

Introduction 7

About This Book 9

Week One:
*Transformed Relationships Are the Seedbed Where
Love Is Planted by the Power of Intention* 19

Week Two:
*Transformed Relationships Thrive in Communities
Where Love Is Grown in an Environment of Grace and
in Relationships of Trust* 43

Week Three:
*Transformed Relationships Remain Vital Only
Where Truth Is Exercised Within the Context of Love
and Integrity of Character Nurtures Trust* 68

Week Four:
*Transformed Relationships Await Us
Along the Journey of Brokenness* 94

Week Five:
*Transformed Relationships Draw Their Strength
to Sustain a Life of Living for Others from the
Fertile Soil of Their Character Rich in Humility* 119

Week Six:
*Transformed Relationships Marked by Acts of Submission Are
the Evidence That One Fully Intends to Love as Jesus Loved* 149

Leader's Guide 177

About the Authors 191

INTRODUCTION

To *experience the life* is to commit to a way or pattern of life. Its basis is humility and it is a life of self-denial and submission to others. The life that Jesus lived and prescribed for us is different from the one being offered by many churches. His servant leadership was radically distinct from what is extolled by secular society and even too bold for what is modeled in the Christian community. This life is essentially the *faith of following*, of taking up one's cross daily and following Him. It is fundamentally about giving up the right to run your own life. It is living the life that Jesus lived, the life to which He has called every disciple.

To put it another way, we can only experience the life Jesus has called us to by committing to training that will enable us to believe as Jesus believed, live as Jesus lived, love as Jesus loved, minister as Jesus ministered, and lead as Jesus led.

It is only by taking Jesus' discipling yoke upon ourselves that can experience the life that Jesus lived. Only then will we discover its light burden and enjoy His promised "rest for our souls" (Matthew 11:29-30).

ABOUT THIS BOOK

This book is the third in the five-book EXPERIENCE THE LIFE series. It continues the thirty-week course, built upon the ideas introduced and developed in Bill Hull's book *Choose the Life,* which begins with the series' first book, *Believe as Jesus Believed.*

Its Purpose

EXPERIENCE THE LIFE exists to assist the motivated disciple in entering into a more profound way of thinking and living. That way is the pattern of life Jesus modeled and then called every interested person to follow. Simply put, it is the living out of Jesus' life by: believing as Jesus believed, living as Jesus lived, loving as Jesus loved, ministering as Jesus ministered, and leading as Jesus led. This *Life* is a life grounded in humility—characterized by submission, obedience, suffering, and the joys of exaltation. It is the life that transforms its adherents and penetrates the strongest resistance. It then calls upon each person to rethink what it means to be a follower of Jesus.

This book is the third in the five-book EXPERIENCE THE LIFE series. It is designed to lead disciples in a thirty-week course, built upon the ideas introduced and developed in Bill Hull's book *Choose the Life.* It provides a daily format that directs a disciple's thinking toward the application of these truths, thereby producing in him a faith hospitable to healthy spiritual transformation—*a faith that embraces discipleship.*

Its Participants

Virtually all significant change can, should be, and eventually is tested in relationship to others. To say that one is more loving without it being verified in relation to others is hollow. Not only do others need to be involved to test one's progress, they are needed to encourage and help someone else in the journey of transformation. Therefore, going on the journey with others is absolutely necessary.

The five books are designed to lead each disciple in a personal journey of spiritual formation by participation within a community of disciples, who have likewise decided to *experience the life*.

The community is composed of (optimally) from two to eight disciples being led in this thirty-week course to *experience the life*.

Participants in the community agree to make time and perform the daily assignments as directed in each book. They have agreed to pray daily for the other members of their community and to keep whatever is shared at their community meeting in confidence. They will attend and fully participate in each weekly community meeting.

Its Process

We recognize that all change, all spiritual transformation, is the result of a process. Events may instigate change in people; they may provide the motive, the occasion, and the venue for change to begin, but the changes that result in healthy spiritual transformation are the product of a process.

We can glean a description of the transformational process from the apostle Paul's command in Romans 12:2:

> Do not conform any longer to the pattern of this world, but be transformed by the renewing of your mind. Then you will be able to test and approve what God's will is—his good, pleasing and perfect will.

This process of transformation asserts that the believer must no longer conform to what is false, the "pattern of this world" (its ideas and values, and the behaviors which express them). Also, he must be transformed, which means his pattern must be changed, conformed to another pattern (the truth), which is not "of this world." This is done by the process of "the renewing of your mind." What does it mean to renew something? To what is Paul referring when he says that the mind must undergo this renewal?

To renew something means to act upon something in ways that will cause it to be as it was when it was new. The principle idea is one of restoring something that is currently malfunctioning and breaking down to its fully functioning state, its original pristine state, the state it was in prior to it sustaining any damage. We must avoid the modern notion that renewing something means simply replacing the old thing with an entirely new thing. Paul, and the people to whom he wrote these words, would simply not understand *renew* to mean anything like what we moderns mean when we use the word *replace*. They would understand that renewing the wheels on one's cart meant repairing them to their fully functioning state. And so, what Paul means by "being transformed by the *renewing* of your mind" (emphasis ours) is that the mind must undergo changes, repairs that will restore it to its original condition, the fully functioning state it enjoyed when it was first created. As these repairs proceed in the restoration/renewal process and a detrimental modification to the original design is discovered, that modification must be removed. It must be removed so that it will not interfere with its operating as it was originally designed. Further, to properly renew anything, we must understand its original design. The best way to renew something is with the direction and assistance of the original builder. A builder in Paul's day was not only the builder but also the designer and architect. With the expertise and help available through the builder, full renewal is best accomplished.

If you are renewing a house, that house's builder would best know how to go about it. If you are renewing an automobile, that automobile's builder would best know how to go about it. In our case, we are renewing the mind. It stands to reason, then, that its renewal would best be accomplished in partnership with its Architect/Builder—God.

We know that it is the mind that is to be renewed, and that we should partner with God to accomplish its renewal, but what is it about the mind that is being renewed? Is it broken, in need of new parts?

When Paul says that it is the mind which is being renewed when spiritual transformation is taking place, he means much more than what most of us think of when we use the word *mind*. Most of us think of the mind as some sort of calculator in our head, so it's understandable that our idea of renewing it would start with the idea of replacing its broken parts. But for Paul, the mind is much more than a calculator in our head, and to renew it means more than simply swapping out a sticky key, or a cracked screen, or replacing the batteries that have run low.

The Greek word that Paul uses and is translated as the English word *mind* is νοῦς. Here it means the inner direction of one's thoughts and will and the orientation of one's moral consciousness. When Paul refers to our mind's renewal, he is saying that the current direction of our thoughts and will must be changed. The way our mind currently directs our thoughts and will no longer leads to where the mind was originally designed to take our thoughts and will. Our mind no longer leads our thinking to know the will of God, to know what is good, pleasing, and perfect, and no longer directs our will to accomplish God's will, to do what is good, pleasing, and perfect. This is in large part what is meant by being lost. If our minds are not renewed, then we cannot live a life directed toward doing what is pleasing to God. We need to undergo the restoration process that will return our minds to operating as they were originally designed, allowing our minds to direct our thinking and will toward God. The good news is that the original Builder/Architect—God—prescribed the renewing of the mind as the sure remedy to restoring us to spiritual health, and He intends to partner with us in this restoration process.

For spiritual transformation to occur there must be a partnership between the Holy Spirit and the person who is to undergo transformation. It is good news that the Holy Spirit is involved in the process of our restoration because, unlike other things that undergo restoration, like houses, tables, and chairs, we are not just passive things. We are more. We are *beings*, *human* beings, *made* in the image of God. Being made in the image of God includes much more than I will (or even can) mention, but for our purposes it includes having thoughts, ideas, passions, desires, and a will of our own. Because these abilities in their current condition (i.e., before renewal) no longer lead us toward God's will, we do not have the ability to direct our own transformation. We need someone who is not "conformed to the pattern of this world," one who is completely conformed to the will of God, to direct the renewal. And because we are in this prerenewal condition, we need someone to initiate, to enable us, and encourage us to continue the process, someone who is not subject to the same problems our condition allows. Who is better to direct than God? Who is better to enable and encourage than God? There is none better suited to the task than the Holy Spirit. That we are partnering with Him is good news indeed!

With the initiating, enabling, and direction of the Holy Spirit, the process of renewal can begin. It is a two-stage process: the *appropriation of the truth* and the *application of truth-directed behavior.* The first stage, the *appropriation of the truth,* takes place when:

1. we have the desire to pursue the Truth to be changed;
2. we then act upon that desire, choosing to pursue the Truth by setting our will.

The second stage, the *application of truth-directed behavior,* takes place when:

1. we begin practicing behaviors, which we'll describe as spiritual disciplines, designed to halt our conformity to "the pattern of this world";
2. we engage in transformational activities, which are designed to reorient our mind and direct it toward God's will;
3. we continue to practice transformational activities to introduce and establish new patterns of thinking and behavior which conform our mind to the mind of Christ.

The same components in the process for renewing the mind that we gleaned from the apostle Paul can also be seen in Jesus' call to anyone who would follow Him.

Jesus commanded to all who would follow Him (all disciples) to:

Come to me, all you who are weary and burdened, and I will give you rest. Take my yoke upon you and learn from me, for I am gentle and humble in heart, and you will find rest for your souls. (Matthew 11:28-29)

Jesus begins with a promise, "Come . . . and I will give you rest." He kindles a desire to follow Him. This is the first step in *the appropriation of truth*, the *desire* to pursue the truth. We *desire* change. Next is Jesus' command to take His yoke. This is the second step in the *appropriation of truth*, *choosing* to pursue the truth. We set our *will* to change. At this step, we can choose to pursue our desire for the truth and change or ignore it. If we choose to delay placing it upon our shoulders it is at the cost of rest to our souls. The choice precedes the action. Next, we read that we are to take His yoke.

To take His yoke is the first step of the second stage in the process of renewing the mind, the *application of truth-directed behavior*. At this step, as we saw before with Paul, we discontinue with our current ways, which conform us to the pattern of this world. We intentionally begin to dislodge the destructive patterns that have grown in us as a precursor to the second step, the taking-upon of a new way, God's way, His yoke.

The second step, the taking-upon of Jesus' yoke, is the part of the process of renewing the mind where the vacancy left from dislodging our old ways, "the pattern of this world," is being filled up with the new life-giving patterns by which we are to conform our lives. It is this yoke, God's new way of living the life that Jesus lived, that is to be taken upon us. Just as the yoke for an ox is placed upon its body, allowing the power of the ox to perform its master's work (work the ox would otherwise not be able to accomplish), so also Jesus' yoke must be placed upon our body to allow it to perform our Master's work, the renewing of our mind (work we would otherwise not be able to accomplish).

Finally, we see the third, and last step, in the *application of truth-directed behavior*. This is the final step in the process of renewal, but it is also the beginning step in the ongoing process of our spiritual transformation. It finally brings us all the way to our taking Jesus' yoke upon us.

It also begins the continuing journey of knowing and doing God's good, pleasing, and perfect will. While the second step trains the mind through establishing patterns, the third step lives out the new character that has replaced the old. This continuing journey begins once we take His yoke upon us. For then we begin to "learn from me [Jesus]" and thereby experience rest for our soul. This rest, this peacefulness that comes from learning from Jesus, is what it is to live with a renewed mind. It is experiencing the Spirit-initiated, encouraged, enabled, and empowered life Jesus enjoyed with the peace that comes only by having the "mind of Christ" and by accomplishing His good, pleasing, and perfect will.

EXPERIENCE THE LIFE provides the disciple a structured process whereby he can engage in the process of spiritual renewal. It provides a daily regimen for practicing specific disciplines designed to displace those old destructive ideas and behaviors (the patterns of the world) and replacing them with new, constructive, life-giving ideas and behaviors (the mind of Christ).

EXPERIENCE THE LIFE requires commitment to consistently practice the disciplines and to reserve the time required for transformation.

Most studies on change agree that displacing a current habit or idea and establishing a new one requires a minimum of about three months. Also, learning studies demonstrate the necessity of consistent application of the thing being learned to ensure its permanent retention.

According to a leading learning researcher, people remember:

- 10% of what they read
- 20% of what they hear
- 30% of what they see
- 50% of what they see and hear
- 70% of what they say
- 95% of what they teach someone else[1]

---

1. William Glassner, *Control Therapy in the Classroom* (New York: Harper and Row, 1986); *Reality Therapy: A New Approach to Psychiatry* (New York: Harper and Row, 1965).

Simply put, we learn best not by passively hearing and seeing, but by actively "doing" the thing which we are learning.

The most relevant question a teacher can ask is, "Are my students learning?" For our purposes, the relevant question must be, "Am I engaged in a process that will result in my being changed from what I am into what I am to be? Am I being transformed into the image of Christ?"

Each book in this series provides a solid opportunity for significant transformation through the use of several common tools or disciplines including:

- Reading Scripture together
- Reading a common philosophy of the Christian experience
- Journaling insights, questions, and prayers
- Discussion over material that has already been studied, prayed over, and reflected upon
- Accountability for the purpose of helping each other keep their commitments to God
- Encouragement to help each other overcome areas of defeat and break free of bondage
- Mutual commitment to apply what God has impressed on each member
- Mutual commitment to impact those with whom they have contact

Its Pattern

This course leads the believer to *experience the life* Jesus lived, utilizing a daily regimen to practice the various spiritual disciplines. The course is thirty weeks long over five books.

The five books, each six weeks in length, instruct and challenge the disciples to conform their life to:

1. Believe as Jesus believed,
2. Live as Jesus lived,
3. Love as Jesus loved,

4. Minister as Jesus ministered, and

5. Lead as Jesus led.

Each six-week book leads disciples through a course of daily teachings and exercises in an examination of how Jesus lived out His faith.

In daily session five, the disciple begins with a prayer focused on the issues to be presented in the daily reading. The daily reading gives a core thought that will be explored in the day's exercises. Questions are designed to help the disciple's understanding of the core thoughts and key ideas. Disciples are then directed to reflect on the application of these core thoughts and key ideas to their own spiritual growth. Journaling space is provided for answering questions and recording thoughts, questions, applications, and insights stemming from their reflection.

Once weekly (the sixth session), the disciple meets with others who comprise their community. At the community meeting they pray together, discuss the core thoughts and key ideas introduced in the week's readings, and share from their own experience of practicing the week's spiritual discipline. They view and discuss the video introduction for the following week's study and pray and encourage one another in their journey of spiritual transformation.

Although the books were designed primarily for use by groups consisting of two to six members, the material and the format can easily be used to effectively lead larger groups in a discussion-based exploration of spiritual transformation.

Lastly, we recommend that the leaders of the weekly discussion groups proceed through each book together as a community group prior to leading their own group. The insights that they will acquire from their own journey through EXPERIENCE THE LIFE will be invaluable to them and the larger group they will lead.

When leading a larger group through EXPERIENCE THE LIFE, keep in mind that most of the spiritual traction for transformation is due to the interaction that the Lord has with each individual through the other individuals in a community of believers. To preserve this traction, the leader must provide a venue and time for this interaction. For this reason, we suggest that some time during the weekly session, the leader divide the large group into smaller groups mimicking the two- to six-member community group for the purpose of more intimately discussing the issues presented in the week's session. It is reported after experiencing successive weeks with the same members of this smaller discussion group individuals previously not participants in a small-group program have desired to continue in such a program.

While we believe that the most effective and efficient means of leading individuals to healthy spiritual transformation is in the context of a smaller community group, we do acknowledge that the larger group setting may be the only means currently available to a church's leadership. Though the *form* of instruction is important, the *function* is what must be preserved: *Verum supremus vultus* (truth above form).

Its Product

Each session is designed to challenge the disciple to examine the progress of his own transformation, to train him with the desire to both know God's will and do it. This course values the spiritual traction the disciple can get by facing this challenge in a high-trust community. Christ was a Man for others. Disciples then are to be people for others. It is only in losing ourselves in the mission of loving others that we live in balance and experience the joy that Christ has promised. And therein lay many of the rewards a disciple may enjoy as he lives and loves as Jesus. This is the life that cultivates Christlikeness and whose product is a transformed disciple — the only life of faith worthy of justifying our calling upon others to Experience the Life.

WEEK ONE

Transformed Relationships Are the Seedbed Where Love Is Planted by the Power of Intention

DAY ONE

Prayer

Dear Jesus, help me to understand what it means for me to love as You loved. Help me to know what You mean by love, and to know what I must do to love others as You do. Amen.

Core Thought

> Love is not a feeling but what we are to do to become like Jesus.

Before we can talk about loving as Jesus loved, we had better make sure we know what we mean by love. The word *love* used to be an excellent word, its meaning understood by nearly everyone. Somehow (and I'm not quite sure when and where) this all changed, and not for the better.

Currently, we use the word *love* to mean: the pleasurable state that you enjoy when you are romantically involved with another person, being "in love." We also use it to refer to feelings that a mother naturally has (or ought to have) for her children. While is it not wrong to use the word love to mean these things, it does diminish love's most important aspect: self-abandonment.

Previously, the word love had nothing at all to do with feeling anything. Love was not considered something that we experience emotionally. Rather, it was an action someone performed to benefit someone else. The translators of the Bible understood love this way and used the word charity in many places in the King James translation for the Greek word for love, *agape*. The chief idea is that love is something you do (actions) to benefit others in recognition of their value. These actions were to be performed without any regard whatsoever for any feelings we have.

By understanding love in the context of charity, we can see that this kind of love is something that has great power. It is God's power for change. It is how God transforms relationships.

Today's Exercises

Core Scripture: John 13:34-35

Read aloud John 13:34-35.

Recite this week's memory verses aloud five times.

> A new command I give you: Love one another. As I have loved you, so you must love one another. By this all men will know that you are my disciples, if you love one another. (John 13:34-35)

Meditate on today's passage.

Request to Be in His Presence

"Dear Lord, bring me into the context of Your world."

1. **Read it**—Remember: We read now only what is there, to hear once again, only what was spoken then. Read John 13:34-35 at least twice, out loud.

2. **Think it**—select a portion, a phrase within the reading, and mull it over in your mind, thinking about the context and setting, reimagining the event, putting yourself into the situation. As you meditate, use all five senses to re-create the context and the setting by building the images that are supplied within the passages.

3. ***Pray it***—ask God to give you understanding into how the truths He has spoken in these Scriptures apply to you now. Ask, "What is it about me that I need to deal with? What is it about me that must change?"

   Respond to God by accepting and admitting whatever responsibility is implied by what He has shown. Write what it is that God has shown you, and what you must admit responsibility for having done (or not done).

4. ***Live it***—ask God to reveal to you what He wants you to do about what you have admitted.

   State what God has revealed that you must admit responsibility for doing.

   State what particular action(s) you will take today to accomplish what God has revealed for you to do.

Discovering the Discipline: Acts of Obedience

Acts of obedience are the evidence of our intention to be Jesus' disciple. "If you love me you will obey my commands" (John 14:15). Clearly then, it is our doing what Jesus commanded that proves we love Him. And what He commanded us to do He has stated very clearly: "A new command I give you: Love one another. As I have loved you, so you must love one another. By this all men will know that you are my disciples, if you love one another" (John 13:34-35). What Jesus is commanding us to do is threefold: we are to do acts of love for one another, to imitate how He loves, and to be recognized as authentic followers of Him because of our acts of love and the way we do them.

This week, we will begin training ourselves to love as Jesus loves. We will engage in practices intended to establish the habits the Holy Spirit will use to transform our current character into one that will authentically respond in obedience to God's will with the same love for others that Jesus has shown.

Doing the Discipline

Today and for the remainder of this week during this time, you will pray, asking the Father to help you to identify one person from among those with whom you live, work, or play to be the recipient of God's love given through your actions. Ask Him for help in keeping your identity a secret as you prepare and then act to make the Father's love for them known.

Journal

Record ideas, impressions, feelings, questions, and any insights you may have had during today's time.

Prayer

Pray for each member of your community.

Transformed Relationships Are the Seedbed Where Love Is Planted by the Power of Intention

DAY TWO

Prayer

Dear Lord, sometimes I get tired of or distracted from (I could give you a list of why I stray) doing what I know I should be doing. Help me to see clearly what it is that is derailing me from continuing to practice the things that will change me into a person that will love others as You do. Amen.

Core Thought

> The power of intention is great and the lack of intention is just as great a power.

Love is God's great power for change. Through love, the Holy Spirit of God transforms our relationships. But we must remember that God cannot transform relationships without also transforming the persons who will have the relationships. Because transformation involves changing a person's mind, understanding, thoughts, values, and desires and changing his choices, will, and actions, it must be done in partnership, in cooperation with the Holy Spirit. So the first step in partnering with God in changing anything about ourselves is to *choose* to do so. This we call our intention. Once we partner the power of our intention with the Holy Spirit's power to change us, our transformation is certain. But before our transformation is certain, we must be certain of our intention.

When William Law witnessed the lives of avowed Christians and how little difference their conduct was affected by their faith, he recognized their condition was due to their lack of intention:

> Why [is it that] the lives of even avowed Christians are thus strangely contrary to the principles of Christianity[?] . . . Now the reason for . . . this [is]: Men have not so much as the intention to please God in all their actions. . . . It is for lack of this intention that you see men who profess religion living in swearing and sensuality—that you see clergymen given to pride, covetousness, and worldly enjoyments. It is for lack of this intention that you see women who profess devotion living in all the folly and vanity of dress and wasting their time in idleness and pleasures. And if you will stop and ask yourself why you are not so devoted . . . your own heart will tell you that it is neither through ignorance or inability but purely because you never thoroughly intended it. . . . Now, who can be reckoned a Christian while lacking this genuine sincere intention? Yet if it generally existed among Christians it would change the whole face of the world. . . . Let a clergyman but have this intention and he will converse as if he had been brought up by an apostle. Let a tradesman . . . and it will make him a saint in his shop. His everyday business will be a course of wise and reasonable actions, made holy to God, by being done in obedience to His will and pleasure. . . . Here is no plea left for ignorance . . . [e]verybody is in the light and everybody has power. And no one can fail except he who is not so much a Christian as to intend to please God.[1]

---

1. William Law, *A Serious Call to a Devout and Holy Life* (Philadelphia: Westminster Press, 1954), 21–23.

Today's Exercises

Core Scripture: John 13:34-35

Read aloud John 13:34-35.

Recite this week's memory verses aloud five times.

> A new command I give you: Love one another. As I have loved you, so you must love one another. By this all men will know that you are my disciples, if you love one another. (John 13:34-35)

Meditate on today's passage.

Request to Be in His Presence

"Dear Lord, bring me into the context of Your world."

1. *Read it* — Remember: We read now only what is there, to hear once again, only what was spoken then. Read John 13:34-35 at least twice, out loud.
2. *Think it* — select a portion, a phrase within the reading, and mull it over in your mind, thinking about the context and setting, reimagining the event, putting yourself into the situation. As you meditate, use all five senses to re-create the context and the setting by building the images that are supplied within the passages.
3. *Pray it* — ask God to give you understanding into how the truths He has spoken in these Scriptures apply to you now. Ask, "What is it about me that I need to deal with? What is it about me that must change?"

Respond to God by accepting and admitting whatever responsibility is implied by what He has shown. Write what it is that God has shown you, and what you must admit responsibility for having done (or not done).

4. ***Live it***—ask God to reveal to you what He wants you to do about what you have admitted.

State what God has revealed that you must admit responsibility for doing.

State what particular action(s) you will take today to accomplish what God has revealed for you to do.

Discovering the Discipline: Acts of Love

Acts of love are the evidence of our intention to become Jesus' disciple.

Our intention to become Jesus' disciple is revealed by our actions in obedience to His command to "love one another." Our intention to become Jesus' disciple means that we intend to do whatever is necessary to establish Him as the only Master we will follow and His way our only way. To become this kind of follower means that we must do what our Master does the way He does it. Simply stated, to love as Jesus loves means that we must do as Jesus does. So if we are to be like our Master we must DO! We must ACT!

Doing the Discipline

Continue to pray to the Father, for help:

- identifying the one person to receive God's love through your actions,

- keeping your identity a secret as you prepare and perform God's act of love, and
- making the Father's love for them known.

Journal

Record ideas, impressions, feelings, questions, and any insights you may have had during today's time.

Prayer

Pray for each member of your community.

Transformed Relationships Are the Seedbed Where Love Is Planted by the Power of Intention

DAY THREE

Prayer

Dear Lord, give me the strength today to be transformed into one who loves as You do. Help me begin to move from merely knowing about what it is in me that must change to acting in the ways that You have prescribed so that I am being changed. Amen.

Core Thought

> By the power of intention we move from merely agreeing about what we ought to find desirable to actually finding what we desire by acting how we ought to.

When our true intention is to please the Father by obeying Him, the real power in our intention can be seen. The power in our intention lies in positioning us beyond simply agreeing that we all need to be changed to admitting that we need to be changed and it must begin now. Once our power of intention takes us this far, the Holy Spirit forms with us a personal partnership for transformation. And once this partnership is formed, the real work to transform us and all our relationships begins.

Today's Exercises

Core Scripture: John 13:34-35

Read aloud John 13:34-35.

Recite this week's memory verses aloud five times.

A new command I give you: Love one another. As I have loved you, so you must love one another. By this all men will know that you are my disciples, if you love one another. (John 13:34-35)

Meditate on today's passage.

Request to Be in His Presence
"Dear Lord, bring me into the context of Your world."

1. **Read it**—Remember: We read now only what is there, to hear once again, only what was spoken then. Read John 13:34-35 at least twice, out loud.
2. **Think it**—select a portion, a phrase within the reading, and mull it over in your mind, thinking about the context and setting, reimagining the event, putting yourself into the situation. As you meditate, use all five senses to re-create the context and the setting by building the images that are supplied within the passages.
3. **Pray it**—ask God to give you understanding into how the truths He has spoken in these Scriptures apply to you now. Ask, "What is it about me that I need to deal with? What is it about me that must change?"

Respond to God by accepting and admitting whatever responsibility is implied by what He has shown. Write what it is that God has shown you, and what you must admit responsibility for having done (or not done).

4. *Live it*—ask God to reveal to you what He wants you to do about what you have admitted.

State what God has revealed that you must admit responsibility for doing.

State what particular action(s) you will take today to accomplish what God has revealed for you to do.

Discovering the Discipline: Acts of Imitation

Acts of imitation are the evidence of our becoming Jesus' disciple.

Our action of loving as Jesus loved is the evidence confirming that we are becoming Jesus' disciple. When we do our acts of love in obedience to Jesus' command we further establish the dominance of His will over our own. When we do these acts of love the way Jesus wants them done, we are establishing within us the dominance of His *values* over our own. It is not merely the doing of what Jesus wants done that transforms us, it is both our doing and our *desiring* that it be done *His way* that transforms us. The desire for having Jesus' will be done His way is grown in us as a result of our imitating the way He did the Father's will the Father's way. This is why Jesus commanded His disciples to "love one another. As I have loved you, so you must love one another."

Imitating Jesus results in our becoming more like Him and less like our former self. Obeying Jesus' commands by imitating Jesus' actions is the way His will becomes dominant in our thinking and His values become dominant in our behavior. Imitation of Jesus' ways causes incorporation of Jesus' will.

Doing the Discipline: Submission to God the Father

Pray, for help

- identifying the one person to receive God's love through your actions,
- keeping your identity a secret as you prepare and perform God's act of love, and
- making the Father's love for them known.

Journal

Record ideas, impressions, feelings, questions, and any insights you may have had during today's time.

Prayer

Pray for each member of your community.

Transformed Relationships Are the Seedbed Where Love Is Planted by the Power of Intention

DAY FOUR

Prayer

Dear Lord, help me today to understand my need to be engaged in relationships whose purpose is to accomplish my transformation. Help me to realize my need to be where my determination to have my own way will be exposed and dealt with. Amen.

Core Thought

> Transformed relationships are the venues where the need to have our own desires fulfilled is transformed by the Spirit's power into the intention to fulfill all that God desires for us to accomplish.

Personal relationships are the venues that the Holy Spirit uses to transform us. Relationships with other people provide us with the opportunities to develop our ability to love others.

If the Holy Spirit is to grow our ability to love, then by definition He will do so by putting us in situations that involve relationships with others. After all, it is impossible to develop our ability to love if we are in isolation. Left alone, we can only develop self-love, and it is obvious that we need anything but development in this area!

But why does the Holy Spirit prefer to use personal relationships to develop our ability to love? Why doesn't He use the affection we have for our pets or the appreciation we have for the grandeur of some majestic scene instead of personal relationships, which are usually so messy? The answer lies in the word "personal."

What the Holy Spirit intends to do ultimately is to restore our ability to fully love God with our whole heart, soul, mind, and strength. And because God is personal, the Father, Son, and Holy Spirit, we will best learn to love Him fully by first learning and practicing our love with other persons. God desires that we know Him personally and that we personally love Him, so He develops our ability to love Him by requiring us to obey His commandment to "love one another as I [Jesus] have loved you."

Whatever else affection for pets and appreciation for scenic grandeur may teach us about God, it will not teach us to love Him as the heavenly Father whom Jesus loved. And they certainly will not train us to prefer another person's desires above our own. For this, the Holy Spirit uses persons who were made in God's own image and who are themselves undergoing the process of having that image restored within them to engage in transformed relationships. This is how He has chosen to form Christ in each of us.

Today's Exercises
Core Scripture: John 13:34-35
Read aloud John 13:34-35.
Recite this week's memory verses aloud five times.

A new command I give you: Love one another. As I have loved you, so you must love one another. By this all men will know that you are my disciples, if you love one another. (John 13:34-35)

Meditate on today's passage.

Request to Be in His Presence
"Dear Lord, bring me into the context of Your world."

1. ***Read it***— Remember: We read now only what is there, to hear once again, only what was spoken then. Read John 13:34-35 at least twice, out loud.

2. ***Think it***— select a portion, a phrase within the reading, and mull it over in your mind, thinking about the context and setting, reimagining the event, putting yourself into the situation. As you meditate, use all five senses to re-create the context and the setting by building the images that are supplied within the passages.

3. ***Pray it***— ask God to give you understanding into how the truths He has spoken in these Scriptures apply to you now. Ask, "What is it about me that I need to deal with? What is it about me that must change?"

   Respond to God by accepting and admitting whatever responsibility is implied by what He has shown. Write what it is that God has shown you, and what you must admit responsibility for having done (or not done).

4. ***Live it***— ask God to reveal to you what He wants you to do about what you have admitted.

   State what God has revealed that you must admit responsibility for doing.

State what particular action(s) you will take today to accomplish what God has revealed for you to do.

Discovering the Discipline: Acts of Love

Acts of love that consistently flow from our own character are the evidence of our having become Jesus' disciple.

Obeying Jesus' command to "love one another" and imitating Jesus way "as I [he] have [has] loved you [us]" is how the Holy Spirit transforms us into Jesus' disciples. Continuing to love as Jesus loved so changes our character to be like His that we more and more gain the ability to respond to others as Jesus did. Our continuing act of loving one another as Jesus loved us is the evidence confirming that we have become Jesus' disciple.

Doing the Discipline

Pray, for help

- identifying the one person to receive God's love through your actions,
- keeping your identity a secret as you prepare and perform God's act of love, and
- making the Father's love for them known.

Journal

Record ideas, impressions, feelings, questions, and any insights you may have had during today's time.

Prayer

Pray for each member of your community.

Transformed Relationships Are the Seedbed Where Love Is Planted by the Power of Intention

DAY FIVE

Prayer

Dear Lord, I've tried to do my best to get along with people and if that wasn't enough, well . . . I just put them behind me and moved on to others. Perhaps I haven't stuck with them as long as I should. What is the right way? Amen.

Core Thought

> To love as Jesus loved we must fully intend to do whatever is required to love as Jesus loved.

To love as Jesus loved requires that we use our power of intention to move beyond agreeing on what is good to entering into a partnership with Holy Spirit to do the will of the One who is Goodness Himself—Jesus. We must not be distracted from doing acts of love by whatever feelings we may have or lack. We must commit to doing whatever it takes for others to be able to receive the love God wants for them to experience through us. To love as Jesus loved, we will love others until they get it. And we will keep on loving others until we finally get it.

Today's Exercises

Core Scripture: John 13:34-35

Read aloud John 13:34-35.

Recite this week's memory verses aloud five times.

> A new command I give you: Love one another. As I have loved you, so you must love one another. By this all men will know that you are my disciples, if you love one another. (John 13:34-35)

Meditate on today's passage.

Request to Be in His Presence

"Dear Lord, bring me into the context of Your world."

1. **Read it**—Remember: We read now only what is there, to hear once again, only what was spoken then. Read John 13:34-35 at least twice, out loud.
2. **Think it**—select a portion, a phrase within the reading, and mull it over in your mind, thinking about the context and setting, reimagining the event, putting yourself into the situation. As you meditate, use all five senses to re-create the context and the setting by building the images that are supplied within the passages.
3. **Pray it**—ask God to give you understanding into how the truths He has spoken in these Scriptures apply to you now. Ask, "What is it about me that I need to deal with? What is it about me that must change?"

Respond to God by accepting and admitting whatever responsibility is implied by what He has shown. Write what it is that God has shown you, and what you must admit responsibility for having done (or not done).

4. *Live it*—ask God to reveal to you what He wants you to do about what you have admitted.

State what God has revealed that you must admit responsibility for doing.

State what particular action(s) you will take today to accomplish what God has revealed for you to do.

Discovering the Discipline: Acts of Love

Acts of love that extend as far as necessary are the evidence that we are Jesus' disciples.

As acts of love become a consistent expression of our obedience to Jesus' commandment, we begin to experience the same freedom Jesus enjoyed, an unfettered ability to fully love another person unconditionally. Acquiring Jesus' ability to love others unconditionally allows us to extend the limits of what we are willing to do to love others as Jesus loves them. The great extent to which we will go to love one another (the determination to love someone until they get it) is the evidence that we indeed love as Jesus loves. It is the final proof of our intention to be Jesus' disciple. When others witness the consistency of our acts of love in imitation of Jesus and the uncompromising extent to which we will go in loving others unconditionally, the only conclusion they can draw is that we are the authentic followers of Jesus. This is what Jesus meant when He told His first disciples that "by this all men will know that you are my disciples, if you love one another."

Doing the Discipline: Submission to God the Spirit
Pray, for help
- identifying the one person to receive God's love through your actions,
- keeping your identity a secret as you prepare and perform God's act of love, and
- making the Father's love for them known.

Journal
Record ideas, impressions, feelings, questions, and any insights you may have had during today's time.

Prayer
Pray for each member of your community.

Transformed Relationships Are the Seedbed Where Love Is Planted by the Power of Intention

Community Meeting

DAY SIX

In preparation for this week's meeting, you will have read and reflected upon each of the week's five Core Thoughts, recorded your thoughts and observations, and are ready to recite this week's memory verses to the group.

WEEK TWO

Transformed Relationships Thrive in Communities Where Love Is Grown in an Environment of Grace and in Relationships of Trust

DAY ONE

Prayer

Dear Lord, help me to desire to be in the kind of relationships that promote my spiritual growth. Help me to reexamine the kind of relationships I'm currently engaged in. Show me which ones to invest in and which ones I should avoid. Amen.

Core Thought

> Love grows best in community, but not all communities will grow love: bad company produces a bad environment, and bad environments reproduce more bad company, ad infinitum ad nauseam.

Love grows best in community. As we saw before, you cannot grow love in isolation. Love requires that there be someone other than ourselves to love. Where there is someone else, there can be community, and if community then there is the possibility that love can grow. But it is only a possibility, not a certainty.

The simple fact that there is a community does not cause love to grow there. In fact, some communities make the growing of love between people all but impossible. These communities have some features in common that are toxic to growing our ability to love. But the single identifiable feature is that they always produce bad company.

Bad company is the quality of the relationships that form when toxic people poison the community they inhabit. Relationships in the environments poisoned by the bad company of toxic people can never be transformational; they can only be deformational. The terrible thing is that while they are incapable of growing love and transforming relationships, bad company seems to cause the best environment for reproducing itself. Bad company results in a bad environment, which in turn produces more bad company to continue the poisoning and deformation of relationships.

To love as Jesus loved requires an environment where love can be practiced so that relationships are transformed.

Today's Exercises
Core Scripture: Ephesians 5:15-21
Read aloud Ephesians 5:15-21.
Recite this week's memory verse aloud five times.

> But the fruit of the Spirit is love, joy, peace, patience, kindness, goodness, faithfulness, gentleness and self-control. (Galatians 5:22-23)

Meditate on today's passage.

Request to Be in His Presence
"Dear Lord, bring me into the context of Your world."

1. *Read it*—Remember: We read now only what is there, to hear once again, only what was spoken then. Read Ephesians 5:15-17 at least twice, out loud.
2. *Think it*—select a portion, a phrase within the reading, and mull it over in your mind, thinking about the context and setting,

reimagining the event, putting yourself into the situation. As you meditate, use all five senses to re-create the context and the setting by building the images that are supplied within the passages.

3. ***Pray it***—ask God to give you understanding into how the truths He has spoken in these Scriptures apply to you now. Ask, "What is it about me that I need to deal with? What is it about me that must change?"

   Respond to God by accepting and admitting whatever responsibility is implied by what He has shown. Write what it is that God has shown you, and what you must admit responsibility for having done (or not done).

4. ***Live it***—ask God to reveal to you what He wants you to do about what you have admitted.

   State what God has revealed that you must admit responsibility for doing.

State what particular action(s) you will take today to accomplish what God has revealed for you to do.

Discovering the Discipline: Being Children of Light

In Ephesians 5:15-17, the apostle Paul teaches us that because we are now "children of the light" we should "be very careful . . . how [we] live . . . [Be] wise, [and] . . . understand what the Lord's will is." "Understanding what the Lord's will is" means not only identifying what it is that the Lord wants us to do but also knowing how He wants us to go about doing it. Paul's word picture of being children of the light is meant to show that we will live like children who are not living in darkness. We can see clearly. We can live according to what God, the Father of Light, has revealed to us. This week we will practice understanding and doing the Lord's will. We will practice being "children of the light."

Doing the Discipline

Last week, you identified one person to be the recipient of God's love given through your actions. Write the first name here _____.

Beginning today and for the next three days during this time, you will pray, asking the Father to tell you how He wants you to show His love to that person. Ask the Father to prepare that person to realize that it is He who is loving them, that they have been on His mind. Ask the Father for wisdom to know what to do and how to do it in a way that will please Him. On day five of this week, you will do what the Father has told you to do to love the person you named above. You will repeat today's discipline each week. You will do whatever the Lord tells you to do that week, to show them His love. You may move the day upon which you do your act of love to whatever day will accomplish it best, but that day must always be preceded by the four days of preparatory prayer.

Journal

Record ideas, impressions, feelings, questions, and any insights you may have had during today's time.

Prayer

Pray for each member of your community.

Transformed Relationships Thrive in Communities Where Love Is Grown in an Environment of Grace and in Relationships of Trust

DAY TWO

Prayer

Dear Lord, I want to do more for You with the life You have given me. I also know that I will not do more for You unless some things about me change. I will work with You on those changes. In the mean time, I want to start being productive for You. Please help me to discover Your abundant life so that I can produce the good things You desire, abundantly. Amen.

Core Thought

Healthy trees produce good fruit from which other healthy trees are grown.

Jesus said, "Make a tree good and its fruit will be good, or make a tree bad and its fruit will be bad, for a tree is recognized by its fruit" (Matthew 12:33). From this we can learn two things that apply to growing love and transforming relationships. The first is that in the same way one is able to make a tree produce either good or bad fruit, we are able to make a person produce either good or bad works.

What Jesus was teaching is that there are things that can "make a tree good," things that will cause a tree to produce its kind of fruit in abundance. Likewise, there are things that will cause people to produce an abundance of works. What is not being taught by Jesus is that you can change the *kind* of fruit a tree will produce. No matter how much you "make a tree good" to enable it to produce its fruit, if it is an apple tree, it will produce its kind of fruit—apples. Likewise, no matter what we do to enable someone to produce an abundance of works, if they are, for example, an evil person, then they will produce an abundance of evil works. They will not produce good works just because they are now enabled to produce more works.

The second thing Jesus taught is that you determine what kind of tree there is by examining its fruit, what it produces. This is very insightful when we consider that the entire future of good fruit depends on the ability to identify and continue to grow only the good trees that produce it. It is only the good trees that will produce the good fruit that contains within it the seeds to grow the next generation of good trees. Likewise, for people to become abundant producers of good works (i.e., loving God by loving others as Jesus loved them), we must do things to enable them to be good people.

In tomorrow's session, we will learn what must be done to make a good people, those who will produce an abundance of good fruit, which will then reproduce according to their own kind.

Today's Exercises
Core Scripture: Ephesians 5:15-21
Read aloud Ephesians 5:15-21.
Recite this week's memory verse aloud five times.

> But the fruit of the Spirit is love, joy, peace, patience, kindness, goodness, faithfulness, gentleness and self-control. (Galatians 5:22-23)

Meditate on today's passage.

Request to Be in His Presence
"Dear Lord, bring me into the context of Your world."

1. *Read it*—Remember: We read now only what is there, to hear once again, only what was spoken then. Read Ephesians 5:18 at least twice, out loud.

2. *Think it*—select a portion, a phrase within the reading, and mull it over in your mind, thinking about the context and setting, reimagining the event, putting yourself into the situation. As you meditate, use all five senses to re-create the context and the setting by building the images that are supplied within the passages.

3. *Pray it*—ask God to give you understanding into how the truths He has spoken in these Scriptures apply to you now. Ask, "What is it about me that I need to deal with? What is it about me that must change?"

Respond to God by accepting and admitting whatever responsibility is implied by what He has shown. Write what it is that God has shown you, and what you must admit responsibility for having done (or not done).

4. *Live it*—ask God to reveal to you what He wants you to do about what you have admitted.

State what God has revealed that you must admit responsibility for doing.

State what particular action(s) you will take today to accomplish what God has revealed for you to do.

Discovering the Discipline: Filling Up on the Spirit

In Ephesians 5:18, Paul teaches that children of the light cannot understand what the Lord's will is if they are filling themselves up with the things that give them a temporary sense of pleasure. Rather, children of the light understand what the Lord's will is by filling up on the Spirit. Paul is commanding us to live our lives according to the Lord's will as it has been revealed to us as the result of our lives being fully occupied by the desire to do the Father's will His way.

Doing the Discipline

Today, continue to pray, asking the Father

- to tell you how He wants you to show His love to this person,
- to prepare that person to realize that it is the Father who is loving them, and
- to give you wisdom to know what to do and how to do it in a way that will please Him.

Journal

Record ideas, impressions, feelings, questions, and any insights you may have had during today's time.

Prayer

Pray for each member of your community.

Transformed Relationships Thrive in Communities Where Love Is Grown in an Environment of Grace and in Relationships of Trust

DAY THREE

Prayer

Dear Father, today help me to pay special attention to my situation. Help me to see how my relationships are either helping me to grow or hampering my growth. Please help me to form my understanding of what I need to do in an environment that helps me to become a disciple who loves others as Jesus does. Amen.

Core Thought

> Growing transformed relationships requires extraordinary attention and a specialized environment.

Yesterday we learned that there are things that can be done that will enable us to love as Jesus loved. Today we will look at another of Jesus' teachings that describes the kind of changes that need to be put in place for us to develop our ability to love as Jesus loved:

> Then he [Jesus] told this parable: "A man had a fig tree, planted in his vineyard, and he went to look for fruit on it, but did not find any. So he said to the man who took care of the vineyard, 'For three years now I've been coming to look for fruit on this fig tree and haven't found any. Cut it down!

Why should it use up the soil?'

"'Sir,' the man replied, 'leave it alone for one more year, and I'll dig around it and fertilize it. If it bears fruit next year, fine! If not, then cut it down.'" (Luke 13:6-9)

In the reading above, Jesus uses this fig tree parable to say that just as the fig tree cannot grow its fruit in conditions that are designed to enable the growth of grapes in a vineyard, likewise we cannot grow the fruit of our new nature in Christ in environments that promote values that oppose the truth, permit sinful behavior, and approve those who gain by so doing.

Jesus teaches that for the fig tree to grow its fruit while it is planted within a vineyard, it must be given special attention: "'Sir,' the man replied, 'leave it alone for one more year.'" The owner had done nothing in three years to enable the fig tree to produce fruit. He was wrong in thinking that where one kind of fruit is produced, it is sufficient for growing another kind of fruit. The people of Jesus' time would have howled in laughter that anyone could be that stupid. An "owner" might be that stupid, they would say (for they tended the vineyards of the rich), but not the Vinekeeper; surely he would know better. And they were right: "I'll dig around it and fertilize it," said the man who tended the vineyard. Here, Jesus teaches that the place, the environment for growing the fruit He desires (love), must be specially prepared. It must be protective to provide us with the security we will need as we begin to establish the roots of our character. It must have the constant attention of the Vinekeeper—the Holy Spirit—to preserve the freedom we need to grow so that the roots of our character can continue to dig deeper, anchoring our faith near reservoirs that will sustain us in times of temptation. Lastly, this special environment must contain the means for monitoring the health of our growth and it must do so by making us accountable for maintaining our commitments to God. These are the people who have our permission to keep track and call us to account for our own growth. They are to tell us, "If it bears fruit next year, fine! If not, then cut it down."

Tomorrow we will identify how to prepare and maintain an environment which will grow us in the grace and love of our Lord, Jesus Christ.

Today's Exercises

Core Scripture: Ephesians 5:15-21

Read aloud Ephesians 5:15-21.

Recite this week's memory verse aloud five times.

> But the fruit of the Spirit is love, joy, peace, patience, kindness, goodness, faithfulness, gentleness and self-control. (Galatians 5:22-23)

Meditate on today's passage.

Request to Be in His Presence

"Dear Lord, bring me into the context of Your world."

1. **Read it**—Remember: We read now only what is there, to hear once again, only what was spoken then. Read Ephesians 5:19 at least twice, out loud.

2. **Think it**—select a portion, a phrase within the reading, and mull it over in your mind, thinking about the context and setting, reimagining the event, putting yourself into the situation. As you meditate, use all five senses to re-create the context and the setting by building the images that are supplied within the passages.

3. **Pray it**—ask God to give you understanding into how the truths He has spoken in these Scriptures apply to you now. Ask, "What is it about me that I need to deal with? What is it about me that must change?"

Respond to God by accepting and admitting whatever responsibility is implied by what He has shown. Write what it is that God has shown you, and what you must admit responsibility for having done (or not done).

4. *Live it*—ask God to reveal to you what He wants you to do about what you have admitted.

State what God has revealed that you must admit responsibility for doing.

State what particular action(s) you will take today to accomplish what God has revealed for you to do.

Discovering the Discipline: Practice Living in the Light

In Ephesians 5:19, Paul tells us to practice various activities to ensure that we continue to be filled with the Spirit, that we continue to live in the light. Doing the things Paul commands enables us to understand the Lord's will. Paul begins by telling us to let the Spirit of God which has filled us up, overflow out of us to bless others. It's Paul's way of saying something like, "just as the drunken man who has filled himself up on wine sings out loud for others to hear, so the children of the light who have filled themselves up with the fruit of the Spirit will sing out." But where the drunk begins the morning sleeping off his stupor in the darkness, the children of the light begin their day in brightness, fully awake and singing praises. Paul is telling us to do as children of the light ought to do. Practice living in the light being filled up with the Spirit. Give praise to others publicly and to God privately.

Doing the Discipline

1. Today, compliment someone by expressing the benefit you have received from them having done some excellent thing or from them having done something ordinary excellently. It would be best if you could do this in a situation where others are present.

2. Take time right now to recall in detail something wonderful that God has done, something that you have witnessed, something that would not have come about except for God taking direct action to accomplish.

3. Continue to pray, asking the Father
   - to tell you how He wants you to show His love to this person,
   - to prepare that person to realize that it is He who is loving them, and
   - to give you wisdom to know what to do and how to do it in a way that will please Him.

Journal

Record ideas, impressions, feelings, questions, and any insights you may have had during today's time.

Prayer

Pray for each member of your community.

Transformed Relationships Thrive in Communities Where Love Is Grown in an Environment of Grace and in Relationships of Trust

DAY FOUR

Prayer

Dear Lord, my natural tendency is to do it myself. I try to rely as little as possible on others to get something done. You know I've been burned when I have counted on others to help me. I need your help to be able to build relationships that require me to trust in someone else. Amen.

Core Thought

> Transformed relationships are established within relationships of trust.

Yesterday we learned that an environment specially prepared, constantly maintained, rich in nutrition, and attentive to our progress is the best way to grow within us the character we need to love as Jesus loved. Today we will talk about the first of two essential qualities that make our environment one that will produce transformed relationships. To transform relationships there must first be relationships of trust.

Relationships of trust provide the foundation for transformational discipleship. Only in trusting relationships can we honestly deal with barriers to obedience and overwhelming sins that hold us back from spiritual growth.

Relationships of trust provide the security that we must be sure is in place for us to feel safe enough to overcome our fear of being truly known by others. In relationships of trust, I feel that I can trust myself to others, that they will not be ones who intend anything but good for me. I feel safe enough to allow them to see me as I am. Within relationships of trust it is okay for me to be just as I am while I am working to become all that I am to be. Relationships of trust make us feel a bit more secure about committing ourselves to being transformed God's way. We are able to say, "Lord, I'm not afraid of Your using [person's name] to make changes in my life."

The result of this vulnerability will reflect what Jesus described: when a student is fully taught, he "will be like his teacher" (Luke 6:40).

Relationships of trust exist where we can answer the question, "Can I trust me with you?" with a resounding yes. Finding at least one person in your life that you can trust provides you with a safe haven of open and honest acceptance. It is there that you can allow yourself to come under that person's influence. Trust is key, because we will only take in the truth we trust. And that trust has to do with the messenger as much as the message. When you trust someone to the point you become vulnerable, you're giving that person permission to speak into your life. This is where transformational traction takes place and from here our progress proceeds.[1]

Today's Exercises

Core Scripture: Ephesians 5:15-21

Read aloud Ephesians 5:15-21.

Recite this week's memory verse aloud five times.

> But the fruit of the Spirit is love, joy, peace, patience, kindness, goodness, faithfulness, gentleness and self-control. (Galatians 5:22-23)

---

1. Bill Hull, *The Complete Book of Discipleship: On Being and Making Followers of Christ* (Colorado Springs: Navpress, 2006), 156–157.

Meditate on today's passage.

Request to Be in His Presence
"Dear Lord, bring me into the context of Your world."

1. **Read it**—Remember: We read now only what is there, to hear once again, only what was spoken then. Read Ephesians 5:20 at least twice, out loud.

2. **Think it**—select a portion, a phrase within the reading, and mull it over in your mind, thinking about the context and setting, reimagining the event, putting yourself into the situation. As you meditate, use all five senses to re-create the context and the setting by building the images that are supplied within the passages.

3. **Pray it**—ask God to give you understanding into how the truths He has spoken in these Scriptures apply to you now. Ask, "What is it about me that I need to deal with? What is it about me that must change?"

   Respond to God by accepting and admitting whatever responsibility is implied by what He has shown. Write what it is that God has shown you, and what you must admit responsibility for having done (or not done).

4. **Live it**—ask God to reveal to you what He wants you to do about what you have admitted.

State what God has revealed that you must admit responsibility for doing.

State what particular action(s) you will take today to accomplish what God has revealed for you to do.

Discovering the Discipline: Practicing Gratefulness

In Ephesians 5:20, Paul instructs us to "always give thanks to God." Today, we train ourselves to be gracious. We will do this by practicing gratefulness.

Begin by listing five common things that God the Father gives you. These are things that God provides throughout the normal course of our lives that don't usually attract our notice, things we take for granted. Some things might include our health, our safety, plenty to eat, a nice view of the mountains, good water, and the ability to see, hear, and smell. Of course, when we take them for granted, we are really taking the One who did them for granted. To love as Jesus loved means not to take what others do for us (indeed, not taking *them*) for granted.

Doing the Discipline

1. Take your list and thank the Father for each of these things. Apologize for not thanking Him for them as much as you know you should. Tell Him how you have enjoyed each of these things, and recall for Him specific instances where experiencing them has given you pleasure. Thank Him for continuing to give you these types of experiences even though you have neglected to thank Him for them. Ask Him to teach you to be more gracious to Him and to others and to train you to express your gratitude, to be gracious, to love others as Jesus loves.

2. Pray, asking the Father
   - to tell you how He wants you to show His love to this person,
   - to prepare that person to realize that it is He who is loving them, and
   - to give you wisdom to know what to do and how to do it in a way that will please Him.

Journal

Record ideas, impressions, feelings, questions, and any insights you may have had during today's time.

Prayer

Pray for each member of your community.

Transformed Relationships Thrive in Communities Where Love Is Grown in an Environment of Grace and in Relationships of Trust

DAY FIVE

Prayer

Dear Lord, I have a tough time feeling gracious toward those who let me down. Sometimes, I let my feelings slip with a little gesture, a rolling of my eyes, or a little comment. It's hard for me to be gracious and encouraging to those who have failed to do what I expected of them. I know it's not right. I need Your help to change. Amen.

Core Thought

> To love as Jesus loved, we must commit to our character being formed in the forge of community and grown within its safe and affirming environment of grace.

Yesterday, we learned that to have transformed relationships there must first be relationships of trust, that trust is key, because we will only take in the truth we trust and will only trust in the truth when it comes from someone we trust. Only when we trust someone to this point can we give that person permission to speak into our lives. And now we can say to God, "Lord, I'm not afraid of Your using [person's name] to make changes in my life. I will listen."

By adding to relationships of trust the second essential quality, which is an environment of grace, the environment for growing transformed relationships is fertile for growing disciples who can love as

Jesus loved. But what does this environment look like?

An environment of grace is a community in which disciples accept each person where they are, celebrate how God has made them, and encourage each other to train to be godly. It is a safe place in which people are encouraged to live out the dream God has for them. An environment of grace is where we are accepted for who we are while we work to become all that we are to be.

An environment of grace is a place we see ourselves and others being affirmed. Affirmation imparts grace; in other words, it is a gift to the recipient. Affirmation is an act of love, and love never arouses sin; instead it arouses the desire to please God.[2] God placed in each of us the need for affirmation, and we are called as a community to meet that need in one another. When I am affirmed in who I am, I don't sit in meetings trying to posture myself to get noticed or to be considered worthy. I am released to minister to others, to focus on how I might help them live out God's dream for them. The happy result is that I can submit to other's strengths and protect their weaknesses.

To love as Jesus loved we must commit ourselves to communities where transformed relationships grow from relationships of trust within environments of grace, where our successes are occasions for celebration, and our failures are occasions for healing, and where every occasion is recognized as an opportunity for forming Christ within us.

Today's Exercises

Core Scripture: Ephesians 5:15-21

Read aloud Ephesians 5:15-21.

Recite this week's memory verse aloud five times.

> But the fruit of the Spirit is love, joy, peace, patience, kindness, goodness, faithfulness, gentleness and self-control. (Galatians 5:22-23)

---

2. Bill Hull, *Choose the Life: Exploring a Faith That Embraces Discipleship* (Grand Rapids, MI: Baker, 2004), 151.

Meditate on today's passage.

Request to Be in His Presence

"Dear Lord, bring me into the context of Your world."

1. **Read it**—Remember: We read now only what is there, to hear once again, only what was spoken then. Read Ephesians 5:21 at least twice, out loud.
2. **Think it**—select a portion, a phrase within the reading, and mull it over in your mind, thinking about the context and setting, reimagining the event, putting yourself into the situation. As you meditate, use all five senses to re-create the context and the setting by building the images that are supplied within the passages.
3. **Pray it**—ask God to give you understanding into how the truths He has spoken in these Scriptures apply to you now. Ask, "What is it about me that I need to deal with? What is it about me that must change?"

   Respond to God by accepting and admitting whatever responsibility is implied by what He has shown. Write what it is that God has shown you, and what you must admit responsibility for having done (or not done).

4. **Live it**—ask God to reveal to you what He wants you to do about what you have admitted.

   State what God has revealed that you must admit responsibility for doing.

State what particular action(s) you will take today to accomplish what God has revealed for you to do.

Discovering the Discipline: Submitting to One Another

Ephesians 5:21 teaches that we are to honor Christ by submitting ourselves to one another. The idea is that we should do acts of love for the sake of those He loves. We are to train ourselves to love as Jesus loves by becoming what He was, a servant of all.

Doing the Discipline

Today, honor Christ by serving up God's gift of love in secret to the person He has chosen.

Journal

Record ideas, impressions, feelings, questions, and any insights you may have had during today's time.

Prayer

Pray for each member of your community.

Transformed Relationships Thrive in Communities Where Love Is Grown in an Environment of Grace and in Relationships of Trust

Community Meeting

DAY SIX

In preparation for this week's meeting, you will have read and reflected upon each of the week's five Core Thoughts, recorded your thoughts and observations, and are ready to recite this week's memory verse to the group.

WEEK THREE

Transformed Relationships Remain Vital Only Where Truth Is Exercised Within the Context of Love and Integrity of Character Nurtures Trust

DAY ONE

Prayer

Dear Lord, I'm not comfortable sharing to begin with, so the idea of sharing things that are uncomfortable makes me doubly anxious. Knowing this about myself makes me realize that I will need Your help to share about myself with others and that they will need me to make themselves feel comfortable when they share about themselves with me. Amen.

Core Thought

> Transformed relationships must be based upon truth and lived in the context of love.

Last week we learned that there must be relationships of trust within environments of grace to allow us to engage in the relationships that God will use to form our character to be like Christ's. This safe, affirming, and nurturing environment is what some call a loving environment, and that is a good description. It is good but not complete.

While it is true that a loving environment is conducive to growth, it is also true that an environment that is merely safe, affirming, and nurturing will grow only whatever is already present. It will grow something well, but it will not change something well. As such, it lacks the impetus for change and remains merely promotional but not transformational.

To change us, for Christ to be formed in us, these transformational relationships must propel us from where and who we currently are to where and who we must become. To do so they must be based upon and directed toward what is true. For there to be transformation there must first be truth.

After there is truth there can be action. It is after truth establishes the direction for change that love compels the manner in which we act to effect the change. Truth establishes the what and love informs us how.

For the remainder of the week, we will learn what it means and how we must live in relationships where transformation is based upon truth and occurs within the context of love.

Today's Exercises
Core Scripture: Ephesians 4:11-32
Read aloud Ephesians 4:11-32.
Recite this week's memory verses aloud five times.

> Speaking the truth in love, we will in all things grow up into him who is the Head, that is, Christ. From him the whole body, joined and held together by every supporting ligament, grows and builds itself up in love, as each part does its work. (Ephesians 4:15-16)

Meditate on today's passage.

Request to Be in His Presence
"Dear Lord, bring me into the context of Your world."

1. *Read it*—Remember: We read now only what is there, to hear once again, only what was spoken then. Read Ephesians 4:21-24 at least twice, out loud.

2. *Think it*—select a portion, a phrase within the reading, and mull it over in your mind, thinking about the context and setting, reimagining the event, putting yourself into the situation. As you meditate, use all five senses to re-create the context and the setting by building the images that are supplied within the passages.

3. *Pray it*—ask God to give you understanding into how the truths He has spoken in these Scriptures apply to you now. Ask, "What is it about me that I need to deal with? What is it about me that must change?"

Respond to God by accepting and admitting whatever responsibility is implied by what He has shown. Write what it is that God has shown you, and what you must admit responsibility for having done (or not done).

4. *Live it*—ask God to reveal to you what He wants you to do about what you have admitted.

State what God has revealed that you must admit responsibility for doing.

State what particular action(s) you will take today to accomplish what God has revealed for you to do.

Discovering the Discipline: Putting on Truth

In Ephesians 4:22-25 we are commanded to put off falsehood and to speak truthfully. We are to put on truth.

This week we will practice disciplines that are designed to take the truths that God has revealed and what we know to be true about ourselves and integrate them into our behavior. Our goal is to train ourselves to live according to truth. We will do this by engaging in behaviors that form the habits of living in this new way. In particular, we will introduce habits for establishing the trait of honesty within our character. The disciplines will address honesty in our dealings with others. They will integrate our duty to live according to the truth, align our personal motivations, and establish the habits of speaking honestly that result in the formation of honesty.

Doing the Discipline

Beginning today, we will resume the practice we began two weeks ago of giving in secret the Father's gift of love to someone He has chosen. So, again, during this time, you will pray, asking the Father to help you to identify a person from among those with whom you live, work, or play to be the recipient of God's love, given through your actions. This week, the person will be someone with whom you are angry (probably from some wrong done to you). This should be someone that you feel has not accepted their responsibility for nor sought to remedy the wrong done to you or any bad feelings that exist between both of you.

As before, ask Him for help in keeping your identity a secret as you prepare and then act to make the Father's love for them known.

Journal

Record ideas, impressions, feelings, questions, and any insights you may have had during today's time.

Prayer

Pray for each member of your community.

Transformed Relationships Remain Vital Only Where Truth Is Exercised Within the Context of Love and Integrity of Character Nurtures Trust

DAY TWO

Prayer

Dear Lord, help me to live in such a way that my actions will communicate to others that I can be trusted. Now Lord, help me to keep the commitments I have made to others so that they will find me trustworthy. Amen.

Core Thought

> Transformed relationships are built upon trust, and we will not trust and accept a message of truth until we can trust that we are truly accepted by its messenger.

Our character can be transformed only after two steps are taken; first, that we believe that our current character is truly lacking of something we truly desire, and second, that we act to make the necessary changes. Fortunately, God helps with both steps. He informs (convicts) us of this lacking and inspires within us the desire to please Him (to change ourselves). Notice, however, that I said He helps us. God helps but does not cause us to believe the truth about ourselves nor cause us to act according to what is true about ourselves. If He simply did cause us to believe and act, then we would have a hard time explaining why we have ever failed to do what we know He wants us to do. Mostly, we fail to do His will because we choose to do otherwise. No further explanation need be given here; we are all familiar enough with this truth. There are, however, times when we find it difficult to even consider the truth God wants us to believe about ourselves.

Because God most often uses other believers to communicate His truth, our relationship with them can be the very thing that either enables or hinders our ability to accept it. Before we can accept the truth someone wants to tell us about ourselves for our own good, we must trust that that person truly values us apart from their own good. I will not value the truth someone wants me to know for my own sake if I do not believe that they value me. I must feel accepted by the messenger before I can accept their message.

For us to trust ourselves to someone, we must believe that we are acceptable to them. The order should not surprise us; we have seen it repeatedly wherever God deals with mankind. To transform us into people who forgive, He offers forgiveness for us to experience, to make us merciful and gracious. He has allowed us to experience His mercy and grace and to make us love one another by first loving us. Tomorrow we will learn how that trust is built.

Today's Exercises

Core Scripture: Ephesians 4:11-32

Read aloud Ephesians 4:11-32.

Recite this week's memory verses aloud five times.

> Speaking the truth in love, we will in all things grow up into him who is the Head, that is, Christ. From him the whole body, joined and held together by every supporting ligament, grows and builds itself up in love, as each part does its work. (Ephesians 4:15-16)

Meditate on today's passage.

Request to Be in His Presence
"Dear Lord, bring me into the context of Your world."

1. ***Read it***—Remember: We read now only what is there, to hear once again, only what was spoken then. Read Ephesians 4:25-27 at least twice, out loud.
2. ***Think it***—select a portion, a phrase within the reading, and mull it over in your mind, thinking about the context and setting, reimagining the event, putting yourself into the situation. As you meditate, use all five senses to re-create the context and the setting by building the images that are supplied within the passages.
3. ***Pray it***—ask God to give you understanding into how the truths He has spoken in these Scriptures apply to you now. Ask, "What is it about me that I need to deal with? What is it about me that must change?"

Respond to God by accepting and admitting whatever responsibility is implied by what He has shown. Write what it is that God has shown you, and what you must admit responsibility for having done (or not done).

4. ***Live it***—ask God to reveal to you what He wants you to do about what you have admitted.

State what God has revealed that you must admit responsibility for doing.

State what particular action(s) you will take today to accomplish what God has revealed for you to do.

Discovering the Discipline: Dealing with Anger

In Ephesians 4:26-27 we are commanded to deal properly and promptly with our anger. Paul uses the phrase "do not let the sun go down on your anger." Letting the "sun go down" was, for residents of the great seaport at Ephesus, slang for allowing a ship to dock safely while the crew slept in their harbor for the night.[1] Paul is commanding us not to allow anger safe harbor within us. We must deal with it promptly. We must use it immediately to call ourselves to act against instances of injustice to others, or it must be dismissed by our extending mercy and grace to those who have injured us.

Doing the Discipline

Today, continue to pray, for help

- identifying the one person to receive God's love through your actions, someone with whom you are angry,
- keeping your identity a secret as you prepare and perform God's act of love, and
- making the Father's love for them known.

---

1. Vernique Condorsett, "Idiomatic Parapsis in Pauline Epistles," *Thesaurus Antiquitatum Sacrarum,* vol xii. 785 sqq., (1911), 114.

Journal

Record ideas, impressions, feelings, questions, and any insights you may have had during today's time.

Prayer

Pray for each member of your community.

Transformed Relationships Remain Vital Only Where Truth Is Exercised Within the Context of Love and Integrity of Character Nurtures Trust

DAY THREE

Prayer

Dear Father, I'm sorry for the times when I have stretched the truth. By that I mean when I have lied. I want to be someone whom people can trust, and I know that my "little" lies and deceptions undermine others' ability to believe what I say . . . actually to believe in me. I don't want to be like this anymore. Help me to build my relationships with others based upon the truth. Help me to develop a great love for living in the truth. Amen.

Core Thought

> Transformed relationships are based upon truth, and we cannot believe in the truth of the message until we can believe that the messenger is truthful.

Once we believe and can trust that we are accepted by someone there remains still another condition that must exist for us to believe that God is using him to speak truth into our lives. We must trust that the messenger is truthful, that he is trustworthy regarding truth.

Determining whether a person can be trusted to be truthful, that he will deliver the message of truth that God wants us to believe, can only be accomplished one way. We can determine a person's trustworthiness regarding the truth by knowing how valuable truth is to them. And we can determine the value truth holds for them by observing to what extent they are willing to suffer personal loss to proclaim, preserve, and promote it. In short, we can tell how valuable truth is to someone by how it affects his or her behavior.

If someone has a history of stretching the truth, this behavior indicates that they value what they gain by deforming the truth more than they value being transformed by the truth. A person who willingly perverts the truth for their own purposes cannot be trusted to speak into anyone's life and certainly is not being used by God to speak into our lives, to accomplish His purposes.

If we cannot trust that someone is trustworthy regarding truth as borne out by his behavior, then we will always entertain strong doubt as to whose purpose his message is serving. Once we doubt the source of the message we need never truly consider its content, and the opportunity for transformation is lost.

If, however, we believe we are valued and accepted by someone and we can believe them to be trustworthy regarding truth, then we will allow them to speak into our life. We will not doubt their purpose for addressing the issues in our life, and will not doubt their being used by God to help us keep our commitments to Him.

As much as it may cause us pain to have someone we know and trust speak the truth to us about ourselves, it will be worth every discomfort we will have experienced if on that day Jesus will say to us, "Well done good and faithful servant. . . . Come and share your master's happiness!" (Matthew 25:23).

Today's Exercises

Core Scripture: Ephesians 4:11-32

Read aloud Ephesians 4:11-32.

Recite this week's memory verses aloud five times.

> Speaking the truth in love, we will in all things grow up into
> him who is the Head, that is, Christ. From him the whole

body, joined and held together by every supporting ligament, grows and builds itself up in love, as each part does its work. (Ephesians 4:15-16)

Meditate on today's passage.

Request to Be in His Presence

"Dear Lord, bring me into the context of Your world."

1. **Read it**—Remember: We read now only what is there, to hear once again, only what was spoken then. Read Ephesians 4:28 at least twice, out loud.
2. **Think it**—select a portion, a phrase within the reading, and mull it over in your mind, thinking about the context and setting, reimagining the event, putting yourself into the situation. As you meditate, use all five senses to re-create the context and the setting by building the images that are supplied within the passages.
3. **Pray it**—ask God to give you understanding into how the truths He has spoken in these Scriptures apply to you now. Ask, "What is it about me that I need to deal with? What is it about me that must change?"

Respond to God by accepting and admitting whatever responsibility is implied by what He has shown. Write what it is that God has shown you, and what you must admit responsibility for having done (or not done).

4. **Live it**—ask God to reveal to you what He wants you to do about what you have admitted.

State what God has revealed that you must admit responsibility for doing.

State what particular action(s) you will take today to accomplish what God has revealed for you to do.

Discovering the Discipline: Being Givers

In Ephesians 4:28 we are commanded to deal with theft. We are to "steal no more." Paul's command is not merely that we should no longer do acts of thievery but also that we should stop enjoying the benefit from the things we have already stolen. Paul is saying to us that until we return the property or restore the value of the property, we are continuing to steal its benefits from its rightful owner. For Paul, a person who continues to enjoy the benefits of anything they acquire by sinning cannot be a true disciple of Jesus. Paul makes it clear that Jesus' disciples are to be givers not takers.

Doing the Discipline

1. Search your home and list the stuff that you have that does not belong to you, stuff that you have "permanently borrowed" from work, family, friends, the library, etc., like office supplies, tools,

dishes, or books. You know, the little (or maybe even the big) stuff that nobody will notice is gone. Estimate how much money you would have spent had you purchased all these "borrowed" items.

2. Consider the following question:
   - Do you believe that God would be pleased with your monetary giving when it is comprised of money you have saved by not having to purchase the items you have stolen?

3. Keep your list (we will need it next week). In the meantime, determine what you should do with all this stuff that isn't yours (and also about the stuff that you already used up: pens, pencils, sticky notes, cleaning supplies, gasoline, etc).

4. Today, continue to pray for help
   - identifying the one person to receive God's love through your actions, someone with whom you are angry,
   - keeping your identity a secret as you prepare and perform God's act of love, and
   - making the Father's love for them known.

Journal

Record ideas, impressions, feelings, questions, and any insights you may have had during today's time.

Prayer

Pray for each member of your community.

Transformed Relationships Remain Vital Only Where Truth Is Exercised Within the Context of Love and Integrity of Character Nurtures Trust

DAY FOUR

Prayer

Dear Lord, I look forward to being someone whom You trust to speak for You into the lives of others. Please train me to be trustworthy in carrying Your truth and to deliver it to whomever You have prepared to hear it. Help me to live with the integrity of character so as not to cause others to dismiss Your words to them because of the way I conduct my life. Transform my life into a testimony to Your truth and an example of Your love. Amen.

Core Thought

> Transformed relationships are the hothouses
> God uses to grow in us the integrity of character
> He will use to grow integrity of character in others.

When we commit ourselves to practice our love for one another within transformed relationships, we have committed ourselves to being transformed into Christlikeness. Our transformation is shaped by having our full self conformed by the truth of God, but we will not be transformed simply by hearing what is true nor by merely doing what is commanded. We become transformed, relationships and all, after we hear the truth, once we intend to change and align our lives according to the truth, when we repent of what is false, and while we do what God has commanded us to do.

This is the long way of saying that what really changes us is doing what the Father has commanded us to do—His will His way. And what He has commanded us to do is to love one another as Jesus loved us.

The transforming process is always the same whether we are talking about changing our thinking, our character, or our relationships. We are changed when we are conformed to the truth. We become conformed to the truth by becoming like the truth. We become like the truth by knowing the truth, we know the truth by learning the truth, we learn through training, we train by practicing, we practice to establish habits, and we establish habits to preset our mind, will, and body to continually behave appropriately. Continually behaving appropriately (i.e., according to what is true—doing God's will His way) incorporates the truth into our lives. Incorporating the truth (God's will) into how we live our lives (His way) is what it means for us to be a person with integrity of character.

When the high value a person places upon truth is consistently evidenced by their behavior, we say that that person has integrity. Their values are fully integrated with their life. When we say that this is an honest person we do not mean merely that they do honest things. We mean that they behave honestly because truth comprises their character. Truth is integrated into the whole of who they are and their behavior reflects the transformation that truth has made upon their character. C. S. Lewis explained this process this way:

> I would much rather say that every time you make a choice you are turning the central part of you, the part of you that chooses, into something a little different from what it was before. And taking your life as a whole, with all your innumerable choices, all your life long you are slowly turning this central thing either into a heavenly creature or into a hellish creature. . . . Each of us at each moment is progressing to the one state or the other.[2]

---

2. C. S. Lewis, *Mere Christianity* (New York: Macmillan, 1952), 72.

We are striving to be the heavenly kind of creature, creatures whose character ("central part") is becoming conformed to the truth and being transformed by the Spirit through his relationships with others, creatures whose transformed character and relationships are being used by the Spirit to form Christ in the character of others.

In summary, our relationships become transformed when we commit ourselves to the practice of loving one another as Jesus loved us in transformational relationships of trust within environments of grace.

Today's Exercises

Core Scripture: Ephesians 4:11-32

Read aloud Ephesians 4:11-32.

Recite this week's memory verses aloud five times.

> Speaking the truth in love, we will in all things grow up into him who is the Head, that is, Christ. From him the whole body, joined and held together by every supporting ligament, grows and builds itself up in love, as each part does its work. (Ephesians 4:15-16)

Meditate on today's passage.

Request to Be in His Presence

"Dear Lord, bring me into the context of Your world."

1. *Read it*—Remember: We read now only what is there, to hear once again, only what was spoken then. Read Ephesians 4:29-30 at least twice, out loud.

2. *Think it*—select a portion, a phrase within the reading, and mull it over in your mind, thinking about the context and setting, reimagining the event, putting yourself into the situation. As you meditate, use all five senses to re-create the context and the setting by building the images that are supplied within the passages.

3. *Pray it*—ask God to give you understanding into how the truths

He has spoken in these Scriptures apply to you now. Ask, "What is it about me that I need to deal with? What is it about me that must change?"

Respond to God by accepting and admitting whatever responsibility is implied by what He has shown. Write what it is that God has shown you, and what you must admit responsibility for having done (or not done).

4. *Live it*—ask God to reveal to you what He wants you to do about what you have admitted.

State what God has revealed that you must admit responsibility for doing.

State what particular action(s) you will take today to accomplish what God has revealed for you to do.

Discovering the Discipline: Building Up with Our Speech

In Ephesians 4:29-30, we are commanded to use our speech to meet the needs of others. Our speech must be used to build up, not to tear down.

Doing the Discipline

Continue to pray for help

- identifying the one person to receive God's love through your actions, someone with whom you are angry,
- keeping your identity a secret as you prepare and perform God's act of love, and
- making the Father's love for them known.

Journal

Record ideas, impressions, feelings, questions, and any insights you may have had during today's time.

Prayer

Pray for each member of your community.

Transformed Relationships Remain Vital Only Where Truth Is Exercised Within the Context of Love and Integrity of Character Nurtures Trust

DAY FIVE

Prayer

Dear Lord, I can tell You right now that I like the idea of being one who speaks into another person's life. However, I also must admit that I don't like the idea as much of someone speaking into my life. I know that this is how You intend to grow me, but my knowing and my liking are two different things. I need Your help to keep my commitment to grow how You want me to grow. Please bring those persons of integrity into my life whose words you will use to transform my character. Amen.

Core Thought

> To love as Jesus loved we must trust and accept the truth spoken in love to us by persons of integrity and develop the integrity of our character such that others can trust and accept the truth we speak to them in love.

For us to love as Jesus loved requires that our current character be transformed from one that primarily acts to satisfy our own desires into one like Jesus' that acts primarily for God to meet the real needs of others. The transformational process that brings about this change in our character is accomplished most effectively when we commit to forming and maintaining transformational relationships with select others for the sake of each other's spiritual formation (maturity). But transformational relationships don't just happen. They are not the kind of relationships which form naturally.

Transformed relationships are both the means and the product of a refining process. To form and maintain them requires a specialized environment where a dedicated community centered around trust and truth provides protection and direction, accountability and affirmation. In this environment God uses us to speak into each other's lives and others to speak into ours. But hearing the truth, even when it is spoken to us in love by a person of integrity, will not transform us.

For truth to change our relationships it must first begin its work on us. God's truth changes us by using the transformational traction that is fostered within transformational relationships, where it is expected that God will speak into our lives through the words of others and through our words into their lives.

To be transformed by God's words requires that we do two things: commit ourselves to being obedient to truth that God says to us through others and commit to becoming someone whom God can use to speak into the lives of others. The first commits us to being changed by God at the hands of others. The second commits us to being changed so that we can be the hands of God for making changes in others.

To love as Jesus loved is to live to love and serve the Father, our neighbor, and one another out of the wholeness of our character produced from within our transformed relationships.

Today's Exercises
Core Scripture: Ephesians 4:11-32
Read aloud Ephesians 4:11-32.
Recite this week's memory verses aloud five times.

Speaking the truth in love, we will in all things grow up into him who is the Head, that is, Christ. From him the whole body, joined and held together by every supporting ligament, grows and builds itself up in love, as each part does its work. (Ephesians 4:15-16)

Meditate on today's passage.

Request to Be in His Presence

"Dear Lord, bring me into the context of Your world."

1. ***Read it***—Remember: We read now only what is there, to hear once again, only what was spoken then. Read Ephesians 4:31-32 at least twice, out loud.
2. ***Think it***—select a portion, a phrase within the reading, and mull it over in your mind, thinking about the context and setting, reimagining the event, putting yourself into the situation. As you meditate, use all five senses to re-create the context and the setting by building the images that are supplied within the passages.
3. ***Pray it***—ask God to give you understanding into how the truths He has spoken in these Scriptures apply to you now. Ask, "What is it about me that I need to deal with? What is it about me that must change?"

   Respond to God by accepting and admitting whatever responsibility is implied by what He has shown. Write what it is that God has shown you, and what you must admit responsibility for having done (or not done).

4. ***Live it***—ask God to reveal to you what He wants you to do about what you have admitted.

State what God has revealed that you must admit responsibility for doing.

State what particular action(s) you will take today to accomplish what God has revealed for you to do.

Discovering the Discipline: Acts of Kindness
In Ephesians 4:31-32, we are commanded to get rid of any desire to harm or have harm come to others. We are to displace those sinful desires by doing acts of kindness.

Doing the Discipline
1. Continue to pray for help
   - identifying the one person to receive God's love through your actions, someone with whom you are angry,
   - keeping your identity a secret as you prepare and perform God's act of love, and
   - making the Father's love for them known.

Journal

Record ideas, impressions, feelings, questions, and any insights you may have had during today's time.

Prayer

Pray for each member of your community.

Transformed Relationships Remain Vital Only Where Truth Is Exercised Within the Context of Love and Integrity of Character Nurtures Trust

Community Meeting

DAY SIX

In preparation for this week's meeting, you will have read and reflected upon each of the week's five Core Thoughts, recorded your thoughts and observations, and are ready to recite this week's memory verses to the group.

WEEK FOUR

Transformed Relationships Await Us Along the Journey of Brokenness

DAY ONE

Prayer

Dear Lord, the whole idea of embarking upon a journey that involves becoming broken is, to say the least, a bit unsettling. Please help me to understand what it is about being broken that would make it something I should greatly desire happening to me. Amen.

Core Thought

> The journey of brokenness is the path of everlasting life.

The very word "brokenness" (whatever it means) sounds like something we should make every effort to avoid. Yet those who have lived long and richly in the faith have said that brokenness is essential to becoming Christlike so much so that Henri Nouwen wrote in his book *The Return of the Prodigal Son* that "it is often difficult to believe that there is much to think, speak or write about other than brokenness."[1] Mark Buchanan wrote in his book *Your God Is Too Safe* that there is one soil that usually withers pride. It is brokenness. He goes on to write that brokenness "molds our character closer to the character of God than anything else. To experience defeat, disappointment, loss—the raw ingredients of brokenness—moves us closer to being like God than

---

1. Henri Nouwen, *The Return of the Prodigal Son* (New York: Image Books, 1994), 53–54.

victory and gain and fulfillment ever can."[2]

This sentiment is consistent among those mature in the faith, that until someone experiences authentic brokenness they cannot be a disciple of Jesus. We must first be broken if we are to love as Jesus loved.

But what are we talking about when we say that one must be broken—experience authentic brokenness? Why must I be broken? And, what is it about me that must be broken? For the remainder of the week, we will discuss brokenness. Tomorrow, we will begin to answer the question "What is 'brokenness'?" by first discussing "Unbrokenness."

Today's Exercises

Core Scripture: Isaiah 53:1-12

Read aloud Isaiah 53:1-12.

Recite this week's memory verse aloud five times.

> Then Jesus said to his disciples, "If anyone would come after me, he must deny himself and take up his cross and follow me. (Matthew 16:24)

Meditate on today's passage.

Request to Be in His Presence

"Dear Lord, bring me into the context of Your world."

1. ***Read it***—Remember: We read now only what is there, to hear once again, only what was spoken then. Read Isaiah 53:1-2 at least twice, out loud.

2. ***Think it***—select a portion, a phrase within the reading, and mull it over in your mind, thinking about the context and setting, reimagining the event, putting yourself into the situation. As you meditate, use all five senses to re-create the context and the setting by building the images that are supplied within the passages.

---

2. Mark Buchanan, *Your God Is Too Safe* (Sisters, OR: Multnomah, 2001), 108.

3. **Pray it**—ask God to give you understanding into how the truths He has spoken in these Scriptures apply to you now. Ask, "What is it about me that I need to deal with? What is it about me that must change?"

   Respond to God by accepting and admitting whatever responsibility is implied by what He has shown. Write what it is that God has shown you, and what you must admit responsibility for having done (or not done).

4. **Live it**—ask God to reveal to you what He wants you to do about what you have admitted.

   State what God has revealed that you must admit responsibility for doing.

   State what particular action(s) you will take today to accomplish what God has revealed for you to do.

Doing the Discipline

1. Last week, you identified one person to be the recipient of God's love given through your actions.
   Write the first name here: _____.

2. Beginning today and for the next three days during this time you will pray, asking the Father to tell you how He wants you to show His love to that person. Ask the Father to prepare that person to realize that it is He who is loving them, that they have been on His mind. Ask the Father for wisdom to know what to do and how to do it in a way that will please Him. On Day Five of this week you will do what the Father has told you to do to love the person you named above.

Journal

Record ideas, impressions, feelings, questions, and any insights you may have had during today's time.

Prayer

Pray for each member of your community.

Transformed Relationships Await Us Along the Journey of Brokenness

DAY TWO

Prayer

Dear Lord, help me to realize and repent of my unbrokenness. With that, give me the strength of conviction to allow me to trust You to break me in exactly the right way at the right time for my benefit. And let whatever is going to happen with me be opportunities for others to see Your grace working in me. Amen.

Core Thought

> Unbrokenness is living a lie.

Unbrokenness is living in a state of denial. It is living a life that denies what is true about God, ourselves, and what we know we ought to be doing (obeying—loving) and ought not to be doing (disobeying—sinning). Unbrokenness is living as if disobeying God (sinning) had no real consequences. It denies the damaging effects my sin has upon me and others. The extent of my unbrokenness is shown by my unwillingness to do something to change the things about me that allow me to continue to harm myself and others. Unbrokenness is a refusal to believe what God says is true and to do what He commands (His will), to live according to that truth (His will His way).

We see the first example of unbrokenness when Adam and Eve chose to believe a lie about God, themselves, and what they knew they ought to be doing (living according to the truth that God had spoken). The harmful consequence of their sin began to appear as surely as they were promised by God.

God had told them that the consequence of living according to their own ways would bring them only death. That living apart from God brings about death is seen in the very way God phrased His commandment to Adam and Eve: "But you must not eat from the tree of the knowledge of good and evil, for when you eat of it you will surely die" (Genesis 2:17). In Hebrew, the last phrase literally means "dying you shall die." This means verse 17 should be understood to mean, "when you eat of the fruit of knowledge of good and evil you will begin dying a certain death." They would, if you will, begin a life that will result only in their death.

Adam and Eve and all who followed would live out their lives suffering the consequences of continuing to reject God's truth and His ways. They would begin to live according to the lies they prefer to believe, seeking to fulfill their own desires. They would live a lie. This is the life of unbrokenness.

Today's Exercises
Core Scripture: Isaiah 53:1-12
Read aloud Isaiah 53:1-12.
Recite this week's memory verse aloud five times.

> Then Jesus said to his disciples, "If anyone would come after me, he must deny himself and take up his cross and follow me. (Matthew 16:24)

Meditate on today's passage.

Request to Be in His Presence
"Dear Lord, bring me into the context of Your world."

1. **Read it**—Remember: We read now only what is there, to hear once again, only what was spoken then. Read Isaiah 53:3-4 at least twice, out loud.

2. ***Think it***—select a portion, a phrase within the reading, and mull it over in your mind, thinking about the context and setting, reimagining the event, putting yourself into the situation. As you meditate, use all five senses to re-create the context and the setting by building the images that are supplied within the passages.

3. ***Pray it***—ask God to give you understanding into how the truths He has spoken in these Scriptures apply to you now. Ask, "What is it about me that I need to deal with? What is it about me that must change?"

   Respond to God by accepting and admitting whatever responsibility is implied by what He has shown. Write what it is that God has shown you, and what you must admit responsibility for having done (or not done).

4. ***Live it***—ask God to reveal to you what He wants you to do about what you have admitted.

   State what God has revealed that you must admit responsibility for doing.

State what particular action(s) you will take today to accomplish what God has revealed for you to do.

Doing the Discipline

1. Take the list you made last week of the items you stole and still have and of items you stole and have since used up or are no longer in possession of, and return the items you still possess to what or whomever is their owner.
2. Items that are no longer in your possession cannot be returned to their owner. However, you can reimburse the owner for what they paid for the item.
3. Seek guidance as to how you will go about returning the items or reimbursing for the items.
   - Ask God how He wants you to do it.
   - Ask other members of your ETL Community for their prayerfully sought recommendations.

Let's be clear, it is no longer a matter of *should* they be returned or reimbursed for, it is only a matter of *when* and *how*. We will take care of the *when* matter now.

4. Return the items and make your reimbursements beginning Day One of Week Five and completed by Day Five.
5. Pray, asking the Father
   - to tell you how He wants you to show His love to this person,
   - to prepare that person to realize that it is He who is loving them, and
   - to give you wisdom to know what to do and how to do it in a way that will please Him.

Journal

Record ideas, impressions, feelings, questions, and any insights you may have had during today's time.

Prayer

Pray for each member of your community.

Transformed Relationships Await Us Along the Journey of Brokenness

DAY THREE

Prayer

Dear Father, give me strength to resist and overcome the temptations of the world's system, the forces of evil, and my own sinfulness. Train me to believe that alone I am powerless to overcome my own sinful will, that I must admit my inabilities, and wholly trust that You will supply whatever is lacking in me to do what is pleasing in Your sight. Help me to truly believe that You will do this for me just because You love me. Amen.

Core Thought

> Unbrokenness is dying to die.

Like it or not, we are all natural-born sinners. We inherited our sin-infected spiritual DNA from our forefather Adam, the first in the long line of sinners. Because of Adam we enter life born able and ready to sin. And unless God intervenes to change our state, we will live out our lives continuing to sin. The word that best describes this condition is unbrokenness.

We are born unbroken. The apostle Paul describes this as living "dead in [our] transgressions and sins, . . . follow[ing] the ways of this world and of the ruler of the kingdom of the air, [according to] the spirit who is now at work in those who are disobedient" (Ephesians 2:1-2).

Those who remain in this unbroken state will continue, like Adam and Eve, to die (remember "dying you shall die" from Genesis 2:17).

This was what we talked about yesterday. Remaining unbroken means that you continue to reject God's truth and continue to believe and live according to what is false. You are living a lie. Those who remain unbroken will have used their years up never having really lived, only continuing their separation from God until they breathe their last and reach their final state, eternal death—dying forever apart from that which would have given them complete satisfaction, God. This is dying to die, existing forever in unbrokenness. The Good News is that God in Christ has reconciled us to Himself. Christ has done everything that we could not do for ourselves to be reconciled to God. He gave us a new kind of life.

Through Jesus, we died to sin. Because of Jesus' perfect life of obedience (doing the Father's will His way) sin could not continue to exercise its corrupting power over Him. His being resurrected from the dead, never to die again, is the evidence that His life of obedience had broken sin's power to bring eternal death to all men. Through Jesus we have been saved from death to begin living out this new, eternal kind of life. He has done for us everything that we could not do to be reconciled to God, and enables us to receive and live out this new eternal life. But Jesus did not do all that we must do to live this new kind of life; after all, Jesus cannot live our life for us. We must live out the life that Jesus won for us.

Jesus has rescued us from the absolute control and the ultimate consequence of sin. However, He has not removed from us the immediate influence and effects of living in a sinful world nor has He removed the immediate consequences of our own sinning. And, unless we do our part (what Jesus has left for us to do) the proper way (according to His will), we will continue to be conformed to this corrupted world's ways. We will, for no other reason than that we choose so, continue living the life of death from which Jesus had already redeemed us. This is what is meant by continuing to live in unbrokenness.

Those who remain unbroken will continue to throw off God's rule over their lives, disobey God's commands, and prefer their own will to His. By doing so they will become more corrupt in their ways and continue to grow the separation that exists between them and the God who loves them. Those who remain unbroken go from bad to worse and from sad to evil, unless they choose to live differently. They will remain unbroken until they are forcibly broken down to forever suffer the anguish of their everlasting unbrokenness.

Tomorrow we will learn about brokenness, what must be broken, and why.

Today's Exercises

Core Scripture: Isaiah 53:1-12

Read aloud Isaiah 53:1-12.

Recite this week's memory verse aloud five times.

> Then Jesus said to his disciples, "If anyone would come after me, he must deny himself and take up his cross and follow me. (Matthew 16:24)

Meditate on today's passage.

Request to Be in His Presence

"Dear Lord, bring me into the context of Your world."

1. ***Read it***—Remember: We read now only what is there, to hear once again, only what was spoken then. Read Isaiah 53:5-7 at least twice, out loud.
2. ***Think it***—select a portion, a phrase within the reading, and mull it over in your mind, thinking about the context and setting, reimagining the event, putting yourself into the situation. As you meditate, use all five senses to re-create the context and the setting by building the images that are supplied within the passages.
3. ***Pray it***—ask God to give you understanding into how the truths He has spoken in these Scriptures apply to you now. Ask, "What is it about me that I need to deal with? What is it about me that must change?"

Respond to God by accepting and admitting whatever responsibility is implied by what He has shown. Write what it is that God has shown you, and what you must admit responsibility for having done (or not done).

4. *Live it*—ask God to reveal to you what He wants you to do about what you have admitted.

State what God has revealed that you must admit responsibility for doing.

State what particular action(s) you will take today to accomplish what God has revealed for you to do.

Doing the Discipline

Continue to pray, asking the Father

- to tell you how He wants you to show His love to the person you have chosen,
- to prepare that person to realize that it is He who is loving them, and
- to give you wisdom to know what to do and how to do it in a way that will please Him.

Journal

Record ideas, impressions, feelings, questions, and any insights you may have had during today's time.

Prayer

Pray for each member of your community.

Transformed Relationships Await Us Along the Journey of Brokenness

DAY FOUR

Prayer

Dear Lord, I don't like to fail. I don't like to be seen as one who fails, and I don't like the feeling I experience when I fail. I don't like anything about failure. You are going to have some job before You to convince me that success in growing my own spiritual maturity is going to be accomplished by my being and admitting that I am a failure. But, if that is what it is going to take . . . If You lead, I will follow. But, please be patient with me; You know I'm going to grumble! Amen.

Core Thought

> Brokenness is dying to live.

Brokenness is the condition that our spirit must be in for God's Spirit to do His transforming work on us and through us. Brokenness is the realization that we are utterly incapable of living the kind of life that will bring us joy, that great enduring sense of fulfillment for which our hearts long. Brokenness begins with the heartfelt admission that I am incapable of being what I want to be. Reaching this stage, becoming broken, is a process, a painful process.

Bringing about in us this heartfelt admission can only be accomplished in one way; we must be made to believe with our whole hearts that we are incapable of succeeding. The only way we will believe this is to believe that despite all our talents, gifts, resources, and good intentions we have wholly failed. All that we are and all that we have have wholly failed to produce all that we want. Of course, for us to believe that we have wholly failed, we must fully experience the pains of failure. And these pains come to us only from having really failed. We arrive at brokenness via failure.

Failure is the perfect tool that God uses to bring us to brokenness. However, our culture has taught us and we have believed that failure is bad. Even with the best spin put upon it, it is only the "best of a bad—well, at least we learned something from it" situation. Spin it as you will, we believe that failure is bad. And, considered in and of itself, we would be correct. But, therein lies the whole problem . . . "in and of itself." God uses our failures to rid us of the problem of "in and of itself."

The very notion that anything can be considered in and of itself exposes the very root of the problem. It is a lie that in God's universe there is anything that can be considered in any way, alone and apart from God (His will being done His way). Determinations about whether failure is a good or bad thing alone, apart from considering what God may be bringing about in any given situation where failure has occurred, are completely unfounded, dehumanizing, and ultimately detrimental. Failure is the tool God uses to prove to us that we cannot succeed in and of ourselves, that by our efforts alone, we will never be all we desire to be. Failure is the tool that God uses to make us abandon hope in our being able to succeed by our own strengths without His help. God uses failure to crush the trust we have in our own abilities. When God crushes our self-trust, we become open to trusting. This is the kind of dying that must take place in us to make room for the Holy Spirit to live out Christ's life through us. This is dying to live.

Tomorrow we will discuss how God uses brokenness to produce in us what He will use to transform us into ones who are able to love as Jesus loved.

Today's Exercises

Core Scripture: Isaiah 53:1-12

Read aloud Isaiah 53:1-12.

Recite this week's memory verse aloud five times.

> Then Jesus said to his disciples, "If anyone would come after me, he must deny himself and take up his cross and follow me (Matthew 16:24).

Meditate on today's passage.

Request to Be in His Presence

"Dear Lord, bring me into the context of Your world."

1. **Read it**—Remember: We read now only what is there, to hear once again, only what was spoken then. Read Isaiah 53:8-10 at least twice, out loud.
2. **Think it**—select a portion, a phrase within the reading, and mull it over in your mind, thinking about the context and setting, reimagining the event, putting yourself into the situation. As you meditate, use all five senses to re-create the context and the setting by building the images that are supplied within the passages.
3. **Pray it**—ask God to give you understanding into how the truths He has spoken in these Scriptures apply to you now. Ask, "What is it about me that I need to deal with? What is it about me that must change?"

Respond to God by accepting and admitting whatever responsibility is implied by what He has shown. Write what it is that God has shown you, and what you must admit responsibility for having done (or not done).

4. *Live it*—ask God to reveal to you what He wants you to do about what you have admitted.

State what God has revealed that you must admit responsibility for doing.

State what particular action(s) you will take today to accomplish what God has revealed for you to do.

Doing the Discipline

Continue to pray, asking the Father:

- to tell you how He wants you to show His love to the person you chose,
- to prepare that person to realize that it is He who is loving them, and

- to give you wisdom to know what to do and how to do it in a way that will please Him.

Journal

Record ideas, impressions, feelings, questions, and any insights you may have had during today's time.

Prayer

Pray for each member of your community.

Transformed Relationships Await Us Along the Journey of Brokenness

DAY FIVE

Prayer

Dear Lord, I want to love others as You love them, and if becoming broken is what it is going to take, then I choose for You to break me. It scares me to think what might happen to me when I know I've just given you permission to do things with me that will cause me to suffer. I know the suffering will be for my good, but just because I know it does not mean that I am looking forward to it. In fact, if it were possible, I wish I could just fast-forward this whole journey quickly past the parts I'm probably not going to like and start enjoying the benefits of having endured them. Yeah, I know it doesn't work that way. Okay then, I'm ready. I choose for You to break me. Go ahead, let's give it a rip! Amen.

Core Thought

> The way of brokenness leads to wholeness.

To love as Jesus loved we must partner with God to transform our relationships into relationships of trust that grow in environments of grace. For us to partner with God we must prefer and accomplish His will over ours. To make it possible for us to prefer His will and ways to our own, He must help us to become wholly dissatisfied with our current manner of living. This is called bringing us to brokenness. He does this through failure. God uses failure to crush the trust we have in our own abilities, opening us up to trusting in His will done His way. This is the kind of dying to ourselves that must take place to make room for the

Holy Spirit to live out Christ's life through us. This is dying to live. But before we can do this God must break us.

God never breaks us as we break things. We break things accidentally or we destroy things in anger or despair. Rarely do we break things in order to improve them. But when God breaks us He does it gently and then puts [us] back together again.[3] It is by God breaking us that we become free to give over to God what we have always valued above all else, control over our own lives. By brokenness God helps us put to death any hope that we thought we had of becoming all that God wants us to be through our own power in our own way.

The psalmist recognized that it is not through our abilities:

> You do not delight in sacrifice,
>> or I would bring it,
>> You do not take pleasure in burnt offerings.

but, through our brokenness, that our relationships (with God and others) are restored and through which our new life begins:

> The sacrifices of God are a broken spirit;
>> A broken and a contrite heart, O God,
>> you will not despise. (Psalm 51:16-17)

The word "broken" used in Psalm 51:17 translates to "crushed, broken in pieces, and torn down," but most importantly, it is also the word used for being "brought to birth"![4] It describes the moment when the mother's water "breaks." It means that two things will now

---

3. Bill Hull, *Choose the Life: Exploring a Faith That Embraces Discipleship* (Grand Rapids, MI: Baker, 2004), 141.

4. Richard Whitaker, Francis Brown, S. R. Driver and Charles A. Briggs, *The Abridged Brown-Driver-Briggs Hebrew-English Lexicon of the Old Testament : From a Hebrew and English Lexicon of the Old Testament by Francis Brown, S.R. Driver and Charles Briggs, Based on the Lexicon of Wilhelm Gesenius*, edited by Richard Whitaker (Princeton Theological Seminary). Text provided by Princeton Theological Seminary, 991.1 (Oak Harbor, WA: Logos Research Systems, Inc., 1997).

certainly happen: first, there will follow much pain and hard labor, and secondly, a new life is about to begin.

God must break us now, so that we will stop living our old life, the life that must be put to death, and begin living the new life He has prepared for us where we experience the life of being transformed disciples growing in transformed relationships who love as Jesus loved.

Today's Exercises

Core Scripture: Isaiah 53:1-12

Read aloud Isaiah 53:1-12.

Recite this week's memory verse aloud five times.

> Then Jesus said to his disciples, "If anyone would come after me, he must deny himself and take up his cross and follow me. (Matthew 16:24)

Meditate on today's passage.

Request to Be in His Presence

"Dear Lord, bring me into the context of Your world."

1. *Read it*—Remember: We read now only what is there, to hear once again, only what was spoken then. Read Isaiah 53:11-12 at least twice, out loud.
2. *Think it*—select a portion, a phrase within the reading, and mull it over in your mind, thinking about the context and setting, reimagining the event, putting yourself into the situation. As you meditate, use all five senses to re-create the context and the setting by building the images that are supplied within the passages.
3. *Pray it*—ask God to give you understanding into how the truths He has spoken in these Scriptures apply to you now. Ask, "What is it about me that I need to deal with? What is it about me that must change?"

Respond to God by accepting and admitting whatever responsibility is implied by what He has shown. Write what it is that God has shown you, and what you must admit responsibility for having done (or not done).

4. *Live it*—ask God to reveal to you what He wants you to do about what you have admitted.

State what God has revealed that you must admit responsibility for doing.

State what particular action(s) you will take today to accomplish what God has revealed for you to do.

Doing the Discipline
Today, give God's gift of love, in secret, to the person He has chosen, the one with whom you are angry.

1. Journal what you experienced as you prepared and then performed your secret act of kindness.
2. Answer the following questions:

    What thoughts first came to mind when this discipline was introduced?

    What do you think your performance of this discipline was supposed to do?

    What do you think it actually accomplished?

Journal

Record ideas, impressions, feelings, questions, and any insights you may have had during today's time.

Prayer

Pray for each member of your community.

Transformed Relationships Await Us
Along the Journey of Brokenness

Community Meeting

DAY SIX

In preparation for this week's meeting, you will have read and reflected upon each of the week's five Core Thoughts, recorded your thoughts and observations, and are ready to recite this week's memory verse to the group.

WEEK FIVE

Transformed Relationships Draw Their Strength to Sustain a Life of Living for Others from the Fertile Soil of Their Character Rich in Humility

DAY ONE

Prayer

Dear Lord, I know that You desire for me to be humble, that You are very displeased with anyone who is prideful. Help me to learn what true humility is, and to train it into my character. Amen.

Core Thought

> Humility is the essential characteristic that allows God to grow His life in us.

"'Tis a gift to be simple, 'tis a gift to be free," says the old Shaker hymn. Its verses capture a way of life that held firm the idea that to become godly one must live rightly. According to the hymn, to live rightly meant to obey God's commands and present yourself to Him and others with no pretenses, just as you were, in simple honesty. To live a life that is pleasing to God requires that we know and believe what is true about ourselves and live according to that truth. There is much good in living this simple and free life.

For God to do His transforming work in and through us, we must first become broken. He uses failure to bring us brokenness. Here, we become free to abandon our own ways and consider His. As we are being broken, God is revealing to us what is true about Himself and about us. Here we begin to accept and believe the truths about us, that God has revealed. Once we are broken by God we can begin to build our trust in Him. This trust building starts the moment we begin the serious work of living according to the truths He has revealed, committing ourselves to do His will His way. Our trust in Him grows as we obey His commands and witness Him working in and through our lives.

Living according to the truths that God has revealed to us about Himself, ourselves, and others is what it means to live in humility. For us to be transformed and for the relationships in which we engage to be transformative requires that within us the essential character trait of humility grows.

This week, we will learn what humility is and does and what we must do to grow this trait in our character.

Today's Exercises

Core Scripture: Philippians 2:3-8
Read aloud Philippians 2:3-8.
Recite this week's memory verses aloud five times.

> All of you, clothe yourselves with humility toward one another, because, "God opposes the proud but gives grace to the humble." Humble yourselves, therefore, under God's mighty hand, that he may lift you up in due time. (1 Peter 5:5-6)

Meditate on today's passage.

Request to Be in His Presence

"Dear Lord, bring me into the context of Your world."

1. *Read it*—Remember: We read now only what is there, to hear once again, only what was spoken then. Read Philippians 2:3 at least twice, out loud.

2. ***Think it***—select a portion, a phrase within the reading, and mull it over in your mind, thinking about the context and setting, reimagining the event, putting yourself into the situation. As you meditate, use all five senses to re-create the context and the setting by building the images that are supplied within the passages.

3. ***Pray it***—ask God to give you understanding into how the truths He has spoken in these Scriptures apply to you now. Ask, "What is it about me that I need to deal with? What is it about me that must change?"

Respond to God by accepting and admitting whatever responsibility is implied by what He has shown. Write what it is that God has shown you, and what you must admit responsibility for having done (or not done).

4. ***Live it***—ask God to reveal to you what He wants you to do about what you have admitted.

State what God has revealed that you must admit responsibility for doing.

State what particular action(s) you will take today to accomplish what God has revealed for you to do.

Discovering the Discipline: Considering Others Before Ourselves

In Philippians 2:3, we are commanded to, "Do nothing out of selfish ambition or vain conceit, but in humility consider others better than yourselves." By this, Paul is telling us how to train ourselves to be humble. When he says to "consider others better than yourselves," he means "better" the same way we mean when we say we like carrots better than corn. We mean that we prefer carrots; we would choose to eat carrots *before* we would choose eating corn. Likewise, Paul is telling us to practice and establish the habit of considering other people's needs before our own. In everything we do we are to consider first of all how to best serve others. By doing this we train ourselves not to believe that we are superior to others, that we are more valuable than they.

This week, we will practice the habit of considering others before ourselves to dislodge the sin of pridefulness. The first step will be to train ourselves not to act or expect to be treated in preferential ways. The second is to treat others in ways that show them that you consider them to be, at the very least, equal in worth to you.

Doing the Discipline

1. Today, take special notice of how you treat those whose job it is to serve you.
   • Speak to food service workers, plumbers, and receptionists with courtesy.

- Remember to look them in the eyes and smile when you speak to them.
- Give them your full attention, listening when they speak.
- Say "thank you" for each thing they do for you, and wish them a good day.

2. Begin returning and reimbursing for the items you have stolen. Continue to record the experience in your journal.

3. Continue the practice of giving in secret the Father's gift of love to someone He has chosen. So, again, during this time you will pray, asking the Father to help you to identify a person from among those with whom you live, work, or play to be the recipient of God's love given through your actions. This week, the person will be someone who is poor. This will be a person for whom you can provide something that they would like but would otherwise do without, because they lack the money. And, as before, ask Him for help in keeping your identity a secret as you prepare and then act to make the Father's love for them known.

Journal

Record ideas, impressions, feelings, questions, and any insights you may have had during today's time.

Prayer

Pray for each member of your community.

Transformed Relationships Draw Their Strength to Sustain a Life of Living for Others from the Fertile Soil of Their Character Rich in Humility

DAY TWO

Prayer

Dear Lord, I want always to be in a position which allows Your grace to work on me and allows it to be available to others through me. Help me not to close myself off from Your transforming grace. Amen.

Core Thought

Without humility, God's grace is closed off from our lives.

Humility, Christ's primary character trait, is ground zero for personal transformation. Without humility, Christ wouldn't have submitted Himself to the Father or made the sacrifice of His own life for the whole world. Without humility, God's grace is closed off from our lives (1 Peter 5:5).

One reason even the very best discipleship plans don't result in transformation is that they don't start with humility. Humility forms the environment and relationships that make transformation possible. But what is humility?

"Humility" and "humble" come from the Latin word *humus*, meaning: "fertile ground . . . the material in soils, produced by the decomposition of vegetable or animal matter and essential to the fertility of the earth."[1] To humble means to "make oneself low, to level a

---

1. *Encyclopedia Britannica Online, Humus, Humble, Humility,* http://www.britannica.com/dictionary?book=Dictionary&va=humus&query=humus.

mountain, to bow down, or to be a person of the earth." It is important for us to remember that just as humility and humble share humus as the root of their meaning, they also share with humus the way and purpose for which they are produced.

Humus, remember, is "produced by the decomposition of vegetable or animal matter." *Humus* is the result of something undergoing the process of dying, and (you have probably already guessed it), the process of producing fertile soil is called humiliation. Likewise, humility and being humble are produced by someone undergoing the process of humiliation (dying).

Humus is produced by God to bring new life to dying earth. Likewise, God breaks us, enabling us to become humble. As we undergo this process of humiliation, we are becoming fertile soil, ready to carry the seeds of God's Word, and accepting our low place, ready to be used by God to bring His life to this dying world.

Today's Exercises

Core Scripture: Philippians 2:3-8

Read aloud Philippians 2:3-8.

Recite this week's memory verses aloud five times.

> All of you, clothe yourselves with humility toward one another, because, "God opposes the proud but gives grace to the humble." Humble yourselves, therefore, under God's mighty hand, that he may lift you up in due time. (1 Peter 5:5-6)

Meditate on today's passage.

Request to Be in His Presence

"Dear Lord, bring me into the context of Your world."

1. ***Read it***—Remember: We read now only what is there, to hear once again, only what was spoken then. Read Philippians 2:4 at least twice, out loud.

2. *Think it*—select a portion, a phrase within the reading, and mull
   it over in your mind, thinking about the context and setting,
   reimagining the event, putting yourself into the situation. As you
   meditate, use all five senses to re-create the context and the setting
   by building the images that are supplied within the passages.

3. *Pray it*—ask God to give you understanding into how the truths
   He has spoken in these Scriptures apply to you now. Ask, "What
   is it about me that I need to deal with? What is it about me that
   must change?"

   Respond to God by accepting and admitting whatever
   responsibility is implied by what He has shown. Write what it is
   that God has shown you, and what you must admit responsibility
   for having done (or not done).

4. *Live it*—ask God to reveal to you what He wants you to do
   about what you have admitted.

   State what God has revealed that you must admit responsibility
   for doing.

State what particular action(s) you will take today to accomplish what God has revealed for you to do.

Discovering the Discipline:
Considering Others Before Ourselves

In Philippians 2:4, Paul commands that, "Each of you should look not only to your own interests, but also to the interests of others." He is teaching us that we must keep in mind what is beneficial for both ourselves and others. The idea here is that I am to seek after things that benefit *both* me and others, not just me. It also is teaching me that I must not do things that will benefit me to another's detriment. What benefits me must not hurt others.

Doing the Discipline

Today, think about things that bring you some sort of benefit. For example, consider the clothes or products that you have purchased. Are the people who labor to produce these products deriving anything near a comparable benefit from your having purchased these products or does the benefit you receive far outweigh whatever benefit they receive? Are there people who have actually suffered while producing the products you are benefiting from? What action can you take to either bring some balance in benefit to these laborers or to alleviate some of their suffering?

Continue to pray to the Father, asking for help in:

- identifying the one person to receive God's love through your actions, someone who is poor,

- keeping your identity a secret as you prepare and perform God's act of love, and
- making the Father's love for them known.

Journal

Record ideas, impressions, feelings, questions, and any insights you may have had during today's time.

Prayer

Pray for each member of your community.

Transformed Relationships Draw Their Strength to Sustain a Life of Living for Others from the Fertile Soil of Their Character Rich in Humility

DAY THREE

Prayer

Dear Father, I desire to be just like Your Son. I want You to prepare me to be available to love anyone You desire to love. Train me so that my character normally responds to life's situations out of the humility You have grown there. Amen.

Core Thought

> Humility is Jesus' core character trait; everything flows from it.

Jesus' core character trait was humility, which manifested itself in submission. If it does not become ours, then how can we believe that we are being transformed into His image? This is the heart of Jesus' life and mission; everything else flows from it. There is no way to read Paul's teaching on this subject and draw any other conclusion:

Let this mind be in you which was also in Christ Jesus, who, being in the form of God, did not consider it robbery to be equal with God, but made Himself of no reputation, taking the form of a bondservant, and coming in the likeness of men. And being found in appearance as a man, He humbled Himself and became obedient to the point of death, even the death of the cross. (Philippians 2:5-8, NKJV)

For us to love as Jesus loved requires we must exhibit the same characteristic humility that Jesus displayed. The apostle Paul teaches that this is accomplished by having Jesus' mind in us.

"*Let this mind* be in you which was also in Christ Jesus," Paul writes (emphasis ours). It is written in the imperative voice so as not to be confused with a suggestion. It is a command. The attitude that Jesus models for us is, therefore, necessary to any relevancy in mission. Today however, "let" usually means something like allow or permit as in, "Let me have a piece of your orange" or "Let the kids play for five more minutes, dear." But we must not understand it so. There was a time when "let" was commonly understood in the much more force-ful sense as with "Let him be crucified!" (Matthew 27:23). It is in this forceful sense that Paul is commanding us. He is saying to us first, "You are commanded to have this mind in you!" Next, he will tell us what "this mind" is.

We are commanded to have the same mind in us, "which was also in Christ Jesus." It is Jesus' "mind" (i.e., the same kind of mind) about which we are being commanded. Instead of "mind," many translations say "attitude" from *phronos*, meaning "mind-set" or "frame of mind." Now, Paul makes very clear what this kind of mind, attitude, or mind-set is that we are to have.

What we find at the very heart of this mind-set are the words, "*being* in the form of God, *did not consider* equality with God some-thing to be grasped" (Philippians 2:6, emphasis added). Paul is saying that because Jesus knew and believed the truth about Who and What He was, it caused Him to think and act the way He did. He thought and acted according to the truth that had formed His character. Jesus knew He was the Son of God the Father and that doing His Father's will was why He was born and what would bring Him and His Father the greatest joy. So the first thing about this mind that we are to have in us is that it is founded and formed according to what is true about us, God, and about doing the Father's will.[2]

---

2. Bill Hull, *Choose the Life* (Grand Rapids, MI: Baker, 2004), 159–161.

Tomorrow we will learn how to have Jesus' mind in us and what happens when we do.

Today's Exercises

Core Scripture: Philippians 2:3-8

Read aloud Philippians 2:3-8.

Recite this week's memory verses aloud five times.

> All of you, clothe yourselves with humility toward one another, because, "God opposes the proud but gives grace to the humble." Humble yourselves, therefore, under God's mighty hand, that he may lift you up in due time. (1 Peter 5:5-6)

Meditate on today's passage.

Request to Be in His Presence

"Dear Lord, bring me into the context of Your world."

1. ***Read it***—Remember: We read now only what is there, to hear once again, only what was spoken then. Read Philippians 2:5-6 at least twice, out loud.

2. ***Think it***—select a portion, a phrase within the reading, and mull it over in your mind, thinking about the context and setting, reimagining the event, putting yourself into the situation. As you meditate, use all five senses to re-create the context and the setting by building the images that are supplied within the passages.

3. ***Pray it***—ask God to give you understanding into how the truths He has spoken in these Scriptures apply to you now. Ask, "What is it about me that I need to deal with? What is it about me that must change?"

Respond to God by accepting and admitting whatever responsibility is implied by what He has shown. Write what it is that God has shown you, and what you must admit responsibility for having done (or not done).

4. *Live it*—ask God to reveal to you what He wants you to do about what you have admitted.

State what God has revealed that you must admit responsibility for doing.

State what particular action(s) you will take today to accomplish what God has revealed for you to do.

Discovering the Discipline: Considering Others Before Ourselves

Philippians 2:5-6 reads, "Your attitude should be the same as that of Christ Jesus: Who, being in very nature God, did not consider equality with God something to be grasped." Paul commands us not to be distracted from doing whatever it takes to do God's will, by entertaining thoughts about how doing so might affect our status. We are not to give any consideration at all about how our being a servant to others might affect how we might be perceived.

Today, we will practice resisting our natural inclination to preserve our "proper" place, our station compared to others. We will practice not being the center of attention. By center of attention I don't mean just being the person everyone sees because of having done something to draw everyone's attention. I mean being someone who needs to make sure everyone is giving them the consideration they feel is their due.

This person needs to make sure that others are always taking their value into consideration and often takes steps to make sure this is being done. One of the ways we can see this inclination at work in us is when we feel compelled to make sure everyone involved truly understands our position in some matter. It also shows itself in our need to have the last word about any given matter be our own.

Doing the Discipline

1. Train yourselves to ignore the compulsion to always have yourself taken into consideration.
   - Refuse to have your opinion always taken into account.
   - Where it is proper, simply be quiet.
   - Where someone else shares your opinion, let them be the one who voices it.
   - Resist the temptation to make sure that others know that you share an opinion if you think that doing so is likely to reward you with recognition.
   - Don't let the last thing that is said in the presence of others come from your mouth.

- Don't let the final decision that is made by the group be stated by you.
- Refuse to let the last word about any matter be said by you.
- Do not draw attention to yourself as you do any of the things above.

2. Continue to pray to the Father, asking for help in:
   - identifying the one person to receive God's love through your actions, someone who is poor,
   - keeping your identity a secret as you prepare and perform God's act of love, and
   - making the Father's love for them known.

Journal

Record ideas, impressions, feelings, questions, and any insights you may have had during today's time.

Prayer

Pray for each member of your community.

Transformed Relationships Draw Their Strength to Sustain a Life of Living for Others from the Fertile Soil of Their Character Rich in Humility

DAY FOUR

Prayer

Dear Lord, I realize that most of my Christian life has been spent agreeing with the preaching on Sunday morning and then living the rest of the week however I desired. I know that I will never be nor do all that You wish me to be, and I will not experience the abundant life You have for me as long as I continue to do the same-ol'-same-ol'. Please train me, Lord, to have Jesus' mind and character. Amen.

Core Thought

> Humility flows out from us when the mind of Christ operates from within us.

To love as Jesus loves, we must think the way He thinks and act based upon the same values He holds. To do this we must, as Paul commands, have Jesus' "mind in [us]."

Having Jesus' mind in us means more than simply agreeing that what He believes is true. Having His mind in us means that our personal character must direct our thinking and will to produce the same kind of thoughts and actions that Jesus would have were He in our situation.

Paul tells us what Jesus' mind-set is by showing how it affected His will and thoughts, and by what actions His mind produced.

Jesus knew the truth about Himself and His relationship with God His Father and that He was to do the Father's will the Father's way. Having lived according to these truths trained His mind to continue to think in accordance with these truths. Paul is teaching us that if we live according to the truth (about our self and our relationship with our heavenly Father) Christ's mind will be trained into us. We will have Christ's mind in us. Having Jesus' mind in us means that the *way* we think will be different. Our thinking will operate in accordance with the truth and be directed toward what is true. We will desire what is true and want to do what leads to the truth.

With Jesus' mind in us and our thinking being trained to continue according to the truth, directing our will to choose what is good, pleasing, and perfect, we are transforming and renewing our mind. The transformation of our mind brings us freedom. This is what Jesus meant when He said, "If you hold to my teaching, you are really my disciples. Then you will know the truth, and the truth will set you free" (John 8:31-32). We can see this happening by noticing the difference in the way we consider things.

Paul teaches that having the mind of Christ in us transforms our mind into one that is free, no longer bound to have to take into account things that are not true. We can wholly disregard what is false without having to consider them. We don't have to be bogged down "considering." We are free to spend our time and energy doing the Father's will rather than "considering." This is exactly what the apostle Paul meant for us to understand. Paul states that Jesus "did not consider," that instead, He *made* Himself, *took* the form, *came* in the likeness, *humbled* Himself, and *became* obedient to death. No more considering. It is time for acting.

So, the second and third things about the mind we are to have are: that it functions because of the freedom that living according to truth produces, and that its freedom enables us to do the Father's will His way.

Tomorrow, we will look more closely at what Christ's mind in us enables us to do.

Today's Exercises

Core Scripture: Philippians 2:3-8

Read aloud Philippians 2:3-8.

Recite this week's memory verses aloud five times.

> All of you, clothe yourselves with humility toward one another, because, "God opposes the proud but gives grace to the humble." Humble yourselves, therefore, under God's mighty hand, that he may lift you up in due time. (1 Peter 5:5-6)

Meditate on today's passage.

Request to Be in His Presence

"Dear Lord, bring me into the context of Your world."

1. *Read it*—Remember: We read now only what is there, to hear once again, only what was spoken then. Read Philippians 2:7 at least twice, out loud.
2. *Think it*—select a portion, a phrase within the reading, and mull it over in your mind, thinking about the context and setting, reimagining the event, putting yourself into the situation. As you meditate, use all five senses to re-create the context and the setting by building the images that are supplied within the passages.
3. *Pray it*—ask God to give you understanding into how the truths He has spoken in these Scriptures apply to you now. Ask, "What is it about me that I need to deal with? What is it about me that must change?"

Respond to God by accepting and admitting whatever responsibility is implied by what He has shown. Write what it is that God has shown you, and what you must admit responsibility for having done (or not done).

4. *Live it*—ask God to reveal to you what He wants you to do about what you have admitted.

State what God has revealed that you must admit responsibility for doing.

State what particular action(s) you will take today to accomplish what God has revealed for you to do.

Discovering the Discipline:
Considering Others Before Ourselves

In Philippians 2:7, Paul teaches us that we are to have the same attitude as Jesus, which enabled Him to disregard any concern about Himself being recognized as superior to all men and allowed Him to make "himself nothing, taking the very nature of a servant, being made in human likeness." This complete disregarding of Himself allowed Him to be completely focused upon doing the Father's will for our sake. It enabled Him to make His life all about others.

Doing the Discipline

1. Today, practice having an "it's all about others" attitude.
   - Intentionally place yourself in situations that bring out the "it's all about me" attitude, situations where you feel put out, where people are not valuing you as you would like, where your needs are not being met according to your preferences.
   - Intentionally place yourself in the longest, slowest line (at the store, or on the highway).
   - Examine your own feelings as you wait to be served or are trying to reach your destination.
     a. Do you feel angry about having to wait so long?
     b. Do you start to think things about the others who are ahead of you?
     c. What do you feel about someone who may want to cut in line ahead of you? What about behind you?
     d. What are you learning about yourself from the feelings that well up from within you when you are in positions like this, where others are not treating you the way you wish, or are not considering you at all?
2. Continue to pray to the Father, asking for help in
   - identifying the one person to receive God's love, through your actions, someone who is poor,
   - keeping your identity a secret as you prepare and perform God's act of love, and
   - making the Father's love for them known.

Journal

Record ideas, impressions, feelings, questions, and any insights you may have had during today's time.

Prayer

Pray for each member of your community.

Transformed Relationships Draw Their Strength to Sustain a Life of Living for Others from the Fertile Soil of Their Character Rich in Humility

DAY FIVE

Prayer

Dear Lord, I have chosen to be Your servant. And with that to serve anyone You desire to have served. Please let me experience Your love, compassion, and grace, so that I can passionately convey Your love and grace to those whom You have brought me near. Amen.

Core Thought

> To love as Jesus loved we need to enter into a life of humility, a life focused on others.

Having in us the mind of Christ allows us to do things we could not do solely on our own. It gives us the ability to live a different kind of life, a life focused on others. Having Christ's mind in us gives us the ability to love others in the same way that Jesus loves us. We become willing as never before to give our life in service to others. We become able to love others until they get it. We gain the ability not only to desire to put others' needs before our own but also not to have to consider and seek after the many things that can distract us from loving others as Jesus loved. The chief distraction is the preservation and enhancement of how others perceive us.

In Philippians 2:7, the apostle Paul does not say that Jesus made for Himself a bad or notorious reputation; he says Jesus made no reputation for Himself. Now everyone has a reputation, so this doesn't mean that no one had any opinion about Jesus. We know that Jesus was famous in His time; He had thousands of admirers and hundreds of followers. This has more to do with His own mind-set rather than the opinions of those around him. Out of Jesus' inner character flowed humility. He lived based on His own view of Who He was, Who His Father said He was: "This is My beloved Son, in whom I am well pleased" (Matthew 3:17, NKJV). The trust of their relationship overpowered every other opinion and force. It won over who the multitudes of people following Him thought Jesus was, over who His disciples said He was, and over who the religious establishment said Jesus was. These groups considered Him a healer, a marvelous teacher, a worker of miracles, a maverick, and/or a blasphemer. Jesus saw Himself as a servant: "the Son of Man did not come to be served, but to serve, and to give His life a ransom for many" (Matthew 20:28, NKJV).

Paul explains just how far the humility of Jesus' mind-set would take Him, how far His love for the Father and doing His will in loving us would require Him to go. Jesus "humbled himself and became obedient to death—even death on a cross!" (Philippians 2:8). His humility enabled Him to do more for us than was humanly possible; He loved us until we got it.

Just as humility is Jesus' primary character trait, it should be the foundation we build on as we seek to follow Him and be formed into His image. Think of it this way: without humility, there's no submission; without submission, relationships of trust can't exist; without relationships of trust, we won't make ourselves vulnerable; without vulnerability, no one can influence us; and without influence, we won't change.[3]

To love as Jesus loved requires the same humility, the same willingness to be like fertile soil for the use of the Father. The Father will grow Jesus' life in us, and we will find joy in giving and serving. As we do so, God will bless us just as He did Jesus, "*Therefore* [because He

---

3. Bill Hull, *The Complete Book of Discipleship: On Being and Making Followers of Christ* (Colorado Springs: NavPress, 2006), 158.

stooped so low] God has highly exalted Him" (Philippians 2:9, AMP emphasis added).

Today's Exercises

Core Scripture: Philippians 2:3-8

Read aloud Philippians 2:3-8.

Recite this week's memory verses aloud five times.

> All of you, clothe yourselves with humility toward one another, because, "God opposes the proud but gives grace to the humble." Humble yourselves, therefore, under God's mighty hand, that he may lift you up in due time. (1 Peter 5:5-6)

Meditate on today's passage.

Request to Be in His Presence

"Dear Lord, bring me into the context of Your world."

1. **Read it**—Remember: We read now only what is there, to hear once again, only what was spoken then. Read Philippians 2:8 at least twice, out loud.

2. **Think it**—select a portion, a phrase within the reading, and mull it over in your mind, thinking about the context and setting, reimagining the event, putting yourself into the situation. As you meditate, use all five senses to re-create the context and the setting by building the images that are supplied within the passages.

3. **Pray it**—ask God to give you understanding into how the truths He has spoken in these Scriptures apply to you now. Ask, "What is it about me that I need to deal with? What is it about me that must change?"

Respond to God by accepting and admitting whatever responsibility is implied by what He has shown. Write what it is that

God has shown you, and what you must admit responsibility for having done (or not done).

4. *Live it*—ask God to reveal to you what He wants you to do about what you have admitted.

State what God has revealed that you must admit responsibility for doing.

State what particular action(s) you will take today to accomplish what God has revealed for you to do.

Discovering the Discipline: Considering Others Before Ourselves

Philippians 2:8 reads, "And being found in appearance as a man, he humbled himself and became obedient to death—even death on a cross!" Paul is showing that everything Jesus did, even how He appeared on earth when He arrived as a human infant and how He appeared when He died on the cross as a criminal, was done not for Himself but for our sake. The attitude that Paul commands us to have is Jesus' commitment to make His life not about Himself but all about others.

Today, we continue practicing the "it's all about others" attitude. We will consider the way we present ourselves before others.

Doing the Discipline

1. Consider what you are (or will probably be) wearing today. Ask yourself the following questions (write your answers in the space provided):

   a. Does my appearance honor what is honorable? What is it trying to reveal to others, and what is it trying to conceal from others?

   b. Does it serve the One who is to be served? What does it say I expect from You, Lord, and what does it say You can expect from me?

   c. What does my appearance say I believe about myself in relation to others? What does it say others should know about me, and what does it say I may think about others?

   d. How will considering these things affect your appearance today or tomorrow? How about the way you dress for worship at your church?

2. Pray for help:
   - identifying the one person to receive God's love, through your actions, someone who is poor,
   - keeping your identity a secret as you prepare and perform God's act of love, and
   - making the Father's love for them known.

3. Briefly recount what you experienced yesterday when you intentionally placed yourself in the longest line or the slowest lane. What did you learn about yourself?

Journal

Record ideas, impressions, feelings, questions, and any insights you may have had during today's time.

Prayer

Pray for each member of your community.

Transformed Relationships Draw Their Strength to Sustain a Life of Living for Others from the Fertile Soil of Their Character Rich in Humility

Community Meeting

DAY SIX

In preparation for this week's meeting, you will have read and reflected upon each of the week's five Core Thoughts, recorded your thoughts and observations, and are ready to recite this week's memory verses to the group.

WEEK SIX

Transformed Relationships Marked by Acts of Submission Are the Evidence That One Fully Intends to Love as Jesus Loved

DAY ONE

Prayer

Dear Lord, I must confess to You that the idea of being submissive to someone just because I ought to is strange territory for me. I've always given someone the honor that they are due. That's just good manners. I understand that I should not hold it against someone, that I should not disrespect someone, merely for being less capable or gifted. But what I don't get is why giving someone a position of authority over me when they have not earned my respect is a good thing. I obviously do not understand what this submission thing is all about. Help me, Father. Amen.

Core Thought

The heart of Jesus' life and mission is humility.

In my (Bill) book *Choose the Life*, I make this observation about Jesus' life:

Jesus' core character trait was humility, which manifested itself in submission. If it does not become ours, then how can we believe that we are being transformed into His image? This is the heart of Jesus' life and mission; everything else flows from it.[1]

Humility is the foundational character trait that must be built upon as we seek to follow Jesus and be formed into His image. Jesus' humility allowed Him to divest Himself of the rights and privileges of deity and submit Himself wholly to the will and agenda of His Father. Humility allows us to ignore ourselves long enough for God to come near and heal us. Humility is me saying to God, "I know that I am not what I should be, and I know that I am not able to become what I should be." Submission is my saying to God, "I choose for You to change me and for You to change me however You choose." So, there must first be humility for change to be possible. However, change will only be a possibility unless humility drives us to action.

When humility acts, it is called submission. For the remainder of the week, we learn how God conforms us to His image through humility in action: submission.

Today's Exercises
Core Scripture: John 13:1-17
Read aloud John 13:1-17.
Recite this week's memory verse aloud five times.

> Submit to one another out of reverence for Christ. (Ephesians 5:21)

Meditate on today's passage.

Request to Be in His Presence
"Dear Lord, bring me into the context of Your world."

---

1. Bill Hull, *Choose the Life: Exploring a Faith That Embraces Discipleship* (Grand Rapids, MI: Baker, 2004), 159.

1. ***Read it***—Remember: We read now only what is there, to hear once again, only what was spoken then. Read John 13:1-2 at least twice, out loud.

2. ***Think it***—select a portion, a phrase within the reading, and mull it over in your mind, thinking about the context and setting, reimagining the event, putting yourself into the situation. As you meditate, use all five senses to re-create the context and the setting by building the images that are supplied within the passages.

3. ***Pray it***—ask God to give you understanding into how the truths He has spoken in these Scriptures apply to you now. Ask, "What is it about me that I need to deal with? What is it about me that must change?"

   Respond to God by accepting and admitting whatever responsibility is implied by what He has shown. Write what it is that God has shown you, and what you must admit responsibility for having done (or not done).

4. ***Live it***—ask God to reveal to you what He wants you to do about what you have admitted.

   State what God has revealed that you must admit responsibility for doing.

State what particular action(s) you will take today to accomplish what God has revealed for you to do.

Discovering the Discipline: Practicing Submission

John 13:1-2 teaches that we show our love for God by being obedient to His commands.

We train ourselves to obey the Father's commands by practicing obeying the laws His servants have commanded. Jesus said, "If you love me, you will obey what I command" (John 14:15). He has also commanded that "everyone must submit himself to the governing authorities. . . . The authorities that exist have been established by God. . . . Do what is right and he will commend you. For he is God's servant to do you good" (Romans 13:1-4). Obeying those who Jesus has placed in authority over us shows our love for Jesus. It also provides a means for training us to continually obey His commands.

It is hard to train ourselves to obey the Father's commands for several reasons. Perhaps the biggest reason for this is that we don't sense God watching us as we do what we do. This allows us to believe (falsely) that He is not seeing our disobedience and therefore we will not suffer as a result of it. Further, the hope that our disobedience will bring us what we want, and bring it quicker, is stronger than our belief that we will suffer the consequences of disobeying God. This being the case, we need help in training ourselves to be obedient to God's commands. One way to train ourselves to continually obey the Father's commands (especially since we believe that He's not looking and we will get away with disobedience) is to practice being obedient to the commands of those servants that He has placed in authority over us. Not doing so often results in our punishment.

Doing the Discipline

1. Today, you will honor God by training yourself to obey His commandments by practicing law-keeping:
   - keeping the speed limit
   - parking only where the law allows
   - establishing the habit of always signaling prior to turning
   - coming to a full and complete stop where indicated
   - maintaining the proper distance between your vehicle and the car in front of you
   - not performing other tasks while driving
2. Make mental note of how many laws you have become accustomed to breaking.
3. Last week, you identified one person to be the recipient of God's love, given through your actions. Write their first name here:

   _____.

4. Beginning today and for the next three days during this time
   - pray, asking the Father to tell you how He wants you to show His love to that person
   - ask the Father to prepare that person to realize that it is He who is loving them, that they have been on His mind
   - ask the Father for wisdom to know what to do and how to do it in a way that will please Him.
5. On Day Five of this week you will do what the Father has told you to do to love the person you named above.

Journal

Record ideas, impressions, feelings, questions, and any insights you may have had during today's time.

Prayer

Pray for each member of your community.

Transformed Relationships Marked by Acts of Submission Are the Evidence That One Fully Intends to Love as Jesus Loved

DAY TWO

Prayer

Dear Lord, I understand my need to submit to You. Thinking You don't deserve my obedience shows how badly off I really am. Submitting to You is understandable; it means that I must obey You. But when I submit to someone else, am I to obey them? Just how far does this whole submission thing go? A little light on the subject please, Lord. Amen.

Core Thought

> To love as Jesus loved requires that we humbly submit ourselves in obedience to God and commit ourselves to loving others through acts of service.

At this point, it is crucial that we understand that there is a critical difference between submission in general and submission that transforms.

Generally speaking, submission is a choice that someone makes causing another to act in a certain way. This idea is shared by both kinds of submission. The difference lies in who causes the act of submission.

The general kind of submission allows one person to commit someone else to act in a certain way. The chooser causes the other person to submit their behavior to his will. This is forced submission; the kind between, for instance, a kidnapper and their victim. This kind of submission, where one person uses their power to control another person's behavior to benefit themselves, is damnable. It is as contrary to Jesus' example as can be imagined. His condemnation of those who use their power to force others to submit is constrained only by His supernatural grace (see Luke 11:46).

The kind of submission Jesus modeled, the kind that is transformational, is born of true humility of character. It is carefully chosen self-submission. It can only come where the one who chooses to submit is the one who will perform the acts of submission. For submission to be transformational it must be freely chosen; I must choose to submit myself.

Today's Exercises

Core Scripture: John 13:1-17

Read aloud John 13:1-17.

Recite this week's memory verse aloud five times.

> Submit to one another out of reverence for Christ. (Ephesians 5:21)

Meditate on today's passage.

Request to Be in His Presence

"Dear Lord, bring me into the context of Your world."

1. **Read it**—Remember: We read now only what is there, to hear once again, only what was spoken then. Read John 13:3-5 at least twice, out loud.
2. **Think it**—select a portion, a phrase within the reading, and mull it over in your mind, thinking about the context and setting, reimagining the event, putting yourself into the situation. As you meditate, use all five senses to re-create the context and the setting by building the images that are supplied within the passages.
3. **Pray it**—ask God to give you understanding into how the truths He has spoken in these Scriptures apply to you now. Ask, "What

is it about me that I need to deal with? What is it about me that must change?"

Respond to God by accepting and admitting whatever responsibility is implied by what He has shown. Write what it is that God has shown you, and what you must admit responsibility for having done (or not done).

4. *Live it*—ask God to reveal to you what He wants you to do about what you have admitted.

State what God has revealed that you must admit responsibility for doing.

State what particular action(s) you will take today to accomplish what God has revealed for you to do.

Discovering the Discipline: Practicing Submission

John 13:3-5 teaches that we show the full extent of our love for God by submitting ourselves to His servants.

Doing the Discipline

1. Today, you will train yourselves to love as Jesus loved by serving one of the Father's servants. Select someone on staff at the church you attend for whom you can perform an act of service. The act of service you perform should in someway show that you value them (not just the service they perform) and would like to do something for them. A few examples of acts of service are: washing their car, picking up their cleaning, doing one of their daily or weekly tasks for them, or providing a meal for them on one of their particularly busy evenings.

2. Pray, asking the Father
   - to tell you how He wants you to show His love to this person
   - to prepare that person to realize that it is He who is loving them
   - to give you wisdom to know what to do and how to do it in a way that will please Him.

3. Continue yesterday's practice of honoring God by training yourself to obey His commandments by practicing law-keeping.

Journal

Record ideas, impressions, feelings, questions, and any insights you may have had during today's time.

Prayer

Pray for each member of your community.

Transformed Relationships Marked by Acts of Submission Are the Evidence That One Fully Intends to Love as Jesus Loved

DAY THREE

Prayer

Dear Father, I feel a lot better now knowing that submission is something that I must choose, that it cannot be forced upon me. Also, it is a relief to know that submission is something that I do. It is an action that will produce in me the ability to live humbly. I like that. But I'm still going to need help from You to enable me to serve those I don't consider worthy of my submission. I know how bad that must sound to You (it sounds bad to me also). That's why I need Your help. I need to get over it. Amen.

Core Thought

> Submission should first be understood as
> a love word and only after that as an authority word.

When we choose to submit our will beneath God's and enter into relationships where we act in obedience to His command to love one another as He has loved us, we are partnering with God in the process of transforming us by transforming our relationships.

These transformational relationships of submission are God's primary means for meeting our needs, deepening our humility, and opening us up to receiving His love.

Within these relationships, God *is* loving us through others, God is loving others through us, and we are loving God through loving others.

We have become, and are becoming more and more, what God has intended that we should be all along. We are becoming the principal way by which others personally experience God loving them.

We are being transformed into being just like Jesus. We are becoming for others Immanuel, "God with us." It is for this reason that submission should first be understood as a *love* word and only after that as an *authority* word.

You submit to others because you desire to enter into a relationship that benefits you and those around you. Submission doesn't involve someone keeping you in line, but allows someone to help you keep your commitments to God. Submission means saying, "I choose to let others love me."

Of course, without submission three negative things happen: your needs won't be met, you can't practice humility (the very character trait that allows you to submit yourself to God, and others), and you shut out others from loving you.

When you do submit to God and one another and invite them to join with you on the journey, your needs will be met, you will practice humility, and others will be able to love you. This makes you a growing disciple with Christlike character, through whose giving of service God continues to so love the world (John 3:16).[2]

Today's Exercises

Core Scripture: John 13:1-17
Read aloud John 13:1-17.
Recite this week's memory verse aloud five times.

> Submit to one another out of reverence for Christ. (Ephesians 5:21)

Meditate on today's passage.

---

2. Bill Hull, *The Complete Book of Discipleship: On Being and Making Followers of Christ* (Colorado Springs: NavPress, 2006), 159.

Request to Be in His Presence

"Dear Lord, bring me into the context of Your world."

1. ***Read it***—Remember: We read now only what is there, to hear once again, only what was spoken then. Read John 13:6-11 at least twice, out loud.

2. ***Think it***—select a portion, a phrase within the reading, and mull it over in your mind, thinking about the context and setting, reimagining the event, putting yourself into the situation. As you meditate, use all five senses to re-create the context and the setting by building the images that are supplied within the passages.

3. ***Pray it***—ask God to give you understanding into how the truths He has spoken in these Scriptures apply to you now. Ask, "What is it about me that I need to deal with? What is it about me that must change?"

   Respond to God by accepting and admitting whatever responsibility is implied by what He has shown. Write what it is that God has shown you, and what you must admit responsibility for having done (or not done).

4. ***Live it***—ask God to reveal to you what He wants you to do about what you have admitted.

   State what God has revealed that you must admit responsibility for doing.

State what particular action(s) you will take today to accomplish what God has revealed for you to do.

Discovering the Discipline: Practicing Submission

John 13:6-11 teaches that we cannot submit ourselves to Jesus' will until we submit ourselves to Jesus' way.

We train ourselves to submit to God's will by allowing others to serve us their way. It is wonderful to know what God wants us to do to serve Him. It is also a great feeling to know that we are serving Him the way He wants us to serve Him. So of course there is no greater feeling than to know we are serving someone the way Jesus wants them served. On the flip side, there could be little worse than not being allowed to serve who Jesus wants served, Jesus' way. Yet when we refuse to allow others the opportunity to serve us the way Jesus wants them to, we are doing to them what may be the worst thing we could do.

Doing the Discipline

1. Today, we practice submission by
   - always verbally thanking others for their gifts to you
   - never refusing a gift but receiving it with the same graciousness that Jesus would
   - never qualifying our acceptance of their gift whether it is a compliment, a service of some kind, or some item because conditional acceptance of a gift is an insult to the giver, a sinful attempt to keep yourself from owing someone and a means for remaining in the superior position of having others in your debt

- never putting limits upon someone else's graciousness by imposing a limit upon the extent to which you will allow them to express their generosity to you because this demonstrates our unwillingness to submit to its greatness
- practicing extraordinary graciousness in accepting someone's gift of service no matter their reason for doing it and no matter the form it takes
- simply saying that you are blessed by their generosity
- saying in all sincerity, "thank you," and if you can't sincerely mean it, then train to be more gracious by saying it anyway

2. Pray, asking the Father
   - to tell you how He wants you to show His love to the person on the church staff
   - to prepare that person to realize that it is He who is loving them
   - to give you wisdom to know what to do and how to do it in a way that will please Him

Journal

Record ideas, impressions, feelings, questions, and any insights you may have had during today's time.

Prayer

Pray for each member of your community.

Transformed Relationships Marked by Acts of Submission Are the Evidence That One Fully Intends to Love as Jesus Loved

DAY FOUR

Prayer

Father, I like being perceived as being strong and in control. Help me to get over my need to be considered as such by others. Help me to realize the great strength of character required to submit to others without regard to their station in life or their abilities and aptitudes. Help me not to prequalify others before I will consider submitting to them and serving them. Amen.

Core Thought

Without submission we cannot practice humility, without humility we will not allow others to speak into our lives, and without that vulnerability, transformation won't happen.

It is just as impossible to develop the character trait of humility without actually submitting oneself to God and others as it is to learn to swim without ever getting into the water with other swimmers.

When a swimmer submerses himself in water the effects of his own body's weight are lessened allowing him to float on top and swim, gliding through the water. The more time this person spends in the water swimming, the more accustomed he becomes to being in water. By that, I mean that the more he becomes used to being submersed in water, the more he begins to take less and less notice of the water. He no longer fears the water (especially of being in the deep end), and he has become more at home in the water. He becomes more and more mindful of enjoying swimming and less concerned about being in water. He has dislodged the fear-filled fantasy of drowning in water with the joy-filled reality of swimming in water. But joy will not displace fear until the would-be swimmer gets into the water.

To develop humility of character within us, we must submit ourselves to God and others. And, just as becoming a swimmer requires that we get into the water, so also does developing humility in our character require us to submit ourselves to others. Only by entering and thereby becoming vulnerable to the effects that water has upon us can we begin to develop the habits of a good swimmer. Likewise, only by entering into relationships in which we are submitting to others, opening ourselves up and becoming vulnerable to the effects they can have upon us, and allowing them to speak into our lives, can we be changed and grow humility of character.

Without submission we cannot grow deep in humility of character. Without humility we will not allow ourselves to become vulnerable enough to open ourselves to change. We will not dive in and experience joy.

Today's Exercises
Core Scripture: John 13:1-17
Read aloud John 13:1-17.
Recite this week's memory verse aloud five times.

Submit to one another out of reverence for Christ. (Ephesians 5:21)

Meditate on today's passage.

Request to Be in His Presence
"Dear Lord, bring me into the context of Your world."

1. ***Read it***—Remember: We read now only what is there, to hear once again, only what was spoken then. Read John 13:12-14 at least twice, out loud.

2. ***Think it***—select a portion, a phrase within the reading, and mull it over in your mind, thinking about the context and setting, reimagining the event, putting yourself into the situation. As you meditate, use all five senses to re-create the context and the setting by building the images that are supplied within the passages.

3. ***Pray it***—ask God to give you understanding into how the truths He has spoken in these Scriptures apply to you now. Ask, "What is it about me that I need to deal with? What is it about me that must change?"

Respond to God by accepting and admitting whatever responsibility is implied by what He has shown. Write what it is that God has shown you, and what you must admit responsibility for having done (or not done).

4. ***Live it***—ask God to reveal to you what He wants you to do about what you have admitted.

State what God has revealed that you must admit responsibility for doing.

State what particular action(s) you will take today to accomplish what God has revealed for you to do.

Discovering the Discipline: Practicing Submission

John 13:12-14 teaches that no one is a servant more highly regarded and loved by the Father than the one who with so little regard for himself becomes the servant of anyone who loves the Father.

Are you someone who sometimes gives qualified thanks or compliments to someone for something they have given or done for you? A qualified compliment or thanks occurs when thanks or praise is given and with it, some critical observation or assessment is added. For example, you tell someone in the choir that "this morning's anthem was really great . . . except that the organ was too loud and sometimes drowned out the voices" or "Pastor, your message really spoke to my heart this morning, but did you realize that you gave the wrong reference to one of the verses you quoted two times in a row?"

Offering qualified compliments or thanks is most often another way to reassert our superiority over someone else. We want to remind someone that their gift was nice, but its flaws ought to remind them that their ability does not make them better than we are. After all, we want him to know that we appreciate the effort, and that despite its flaws, we will show him that we're big enough to overlook the flaws and thank him despite them. We are not ignorant; We are knowledgeable: "I am still better than you . . . but thanks for the effort anyway."

To combat our sick need to maintain our superiority over others, we must train ourselves to stop acting to satisfy our compulsion to be esteemed as better than others.

Doing the Discipline

1. Today, practice submission by
   - always verbally thanking others for their gifts to you
   - never refusing a gift but receiving it with the same graciousness that Jesus would
   - never qualifying our acceptance of their gift whether it is a compliment, a service, or an item because conditional acceptance of a gift is an insult to the giver, a sinful attempt to keep yourself from owing someone, and a means for remaining in the superior position of having others in your debt
   - never putting limits upon someone else's graciousness by imposing a limit upon the extent to which you will allow them to express their generosity to you because this demonstrates our unwillingness to submit to its greatness
   - practicing extraordinary graciousness in accepting someone's gift of service no matter their reason for doing it and no matter the form it takes
   - simply saying that you are blessed by their generosity
   - saying in all sincerity, "thank you," and if you can't sincerely mean it, then train to be more gracious by saying it anyway
2. Pray, asking the Father
   - to tell you how He wants you to show His love to the person on the church staff
   - to prepare that person to realize that it is He who is loving them
   - to give you wisdom to know what to do and how to do it in a way that will please Him

Journal

Record ideas, impressions, feelings, questions, and any insights you may have had during today's time.

Prayer

Pray for each member of your community.

Transformed Relationships Marked by Acts of Submission Are the Evidence That One Fully Intends to Love as Jesus Loved

DAY FIVE

Prayer

Dear Lord, I desire to be greatly used by You. I want to be Your cherished instrument for sharing Your life with others. I want to be used to speak into the lives of Your children. I want to be known for my eagerness to serve You. I want to bring relief and healing to those to whom You wish to extend Your grace. I choose to submit myself to You. I choose to become Your servant. I choose to love as Jesus loved. Amen.

Core Thought

> To love as Jesus loved we must show ourselves to be in submission to Christ by submitting to those that comprise His body, the community of Christ.

Yesterday, our swimming analogy helped to show the necessity of submission and becoming vulnerable for personal transformation to occur. Today, however, the analogy begins to fail us. The swimming analogy falls short because while it is possible (though ill-advised) for someone to swim in water with no one else, it is impossible to grow humility of character by being in submission to no one else. In fact, even if it were possible it would still be ill-advised. (I have a sneaking suspicion, though, that even swimming was never intended to be a solo affair. We have probably wrongly made it so. Consider for a second that most swimming naturally occurs in schools. Where it doesn't, it is usually being done by a predator or by one who is about to become its prey! Perhaps we should relearn the virtues of swimming in schools!) Nevertheless, the important point is that submission requires that there be someone other than ourselves to whom we will be submitted. Fortunately, God has provided for us the proper ones to whom we should be submitted.

It is to Christ that we are to be in submission. He is the "other" to whom we must be submitted. More specifically, we are to be in submission to Him by being in submission to His body, the church, those who comprise the members of His body. Paul commands us to "submit to one another out of reverence for Christ" (Ephesians 5:21). In Ephesians 5:1, he refers to the body as "dearly loved children" of God.

To love as Jesus loved, we must be in submission to this community of Christ to do a specific thing for a specific purpose. We are to do whatever is required to be transformed into the image of Christ for the purpose of being Christ present in the world, to reconcile the world to the Father. This will be accomplished by each member of Jesus' body loving each other as Jesus did until they get it and by loving their neighbors with the same unselfish care as Jesus showed.

Today's Exercises
Core Scripture: John 13:1-17
Read aloud John 13:1-17.
Recite this week's memory verse aloud five times.

Submit to one another out of reverence for Christ. (Ephesians 5:21)

Meditate on today's passage.

Request to Be in His Presence
"Dear Lord, bring me into the context of Your world."

1. ***Read it***—Remember: We read now only what is there, to hear once again, only what was spoken then. Read John 13:15-17 at least twice, out loud.

2. ***Think it***—select a portion, a phrase within the reading, and mull it over in your mind, thinking about the context and setting, reimagining the event, putting yourself into the situation. As you meditate, use all five senses to re-create the context and the setting by building the images that are supplied within the passages.

3. ***Pray it***—ask God to give you understanding into how the truths He has spoken in these Scriptures apply to you now. Ask, "What is it about me that I need to deal with? What is it about me that must change?"

Respond to God by accepting and admitting whatever responsibility is implied by what He has shown. Write what it is that God has shown you, and what you must admit responsibility for having done (or not done).

4. ***Live it***—ask God to reveal to you what He wants you to do about what you have admitted.

State what God has revealed that you must admit responsibility for doing.

State what particular action(s) you will take today to accomplish what God has revealed for you to do.

Discovering the Discipline: Practicing Submission

John 13:15-17 teaches that we cannot receive the blessings of God if we continue to seek after them in the same way that those of this world seek after the things they desire.

We train ourselves to be open to God's blessings by refusing to let our previous experiences and current understanding about how God operates restrict the manner in which we will receive His future blessings. When we serve others in the way that the Father is leading us and allow others the blessing of serving us as the Father is leading them, we train ourselves to love as Jesus loved. When we love as Jesus loved, we become open and able to receive the torrent of blessings He wants to drench upon us from the floodgates of heaven.

Doing the Discipline

Today, give God's gift of love in secret to the person on the church staff He has chosen.

Journal

Record ideas, impressions, feelings, questions, and any insights you may have had during today's time.

Prayer

Pray for each member of your community.

Transformed Relationships Marked by Acts of Submission Are the Evidence That One Fully Intends to Love as Jesus Loved

Community Meeting

DAY SIX

In preparation for this week's meeting, you will have read and reflected upon each of the week's five Core Thoughts, recorded your thoughts and observations, and are ready to recite this week's memory verse to the group.

LEADER'S
GUIDE

WEEK ONE

Transformed Relationships Are the Seedbed Where Love Is Planted by the Power of Intention

Community Meeting

DAY SIX

In preparation for this week's meeting, you will have read and reflected upon each of the week's five Core Thoughts, recorded your thoughts and observations, and are ready to recite this week's memory verses to the group.

At This Week's Meeting

1. Open this session by asking God to help each one be aware of His gracious presence.
2. Have each member take their turn reciting to the group this week's memory verses.
3. Discuss this week's Core Thoughts, that:
   a. love is not a feeling but *what we are to do* to become like Jesus,
   b. the power of intention is great, and the lack of intention is just as great a power,
   c. by the power of intention we move from merely indicating what we ought to find desirable to actually finding what we desire by acting how we ought to,
   d. transformed relationships are the venues where the need to have our own desires fulfilled is transformed by the Spirit's power into the intention to fulfill all that God desires for us to accomplish, and

e. to love as Jesus loved we must fully intend to do whatever is required to love as Jesus loved.

4. Allow members to briefly share any insights, questions, or illumination they have resulting from this week's daily readings and exercises.

Experience the Life

5. Play the ETL Course DVD "Book Three: Love as Jesus Loved," "Week 2: Community."

Discussion Questions

6. As a group, discuss the ideas that Bill Hull introduced, and answer the questions below.

Why is it that when we feel safe with other people we are more apt to be trusting and become real in their presence?

Close

Share matters for the community to pray about through the following week. Pray to close the meeting.

WEEK TWO

Transformed Relationships Thrive in Communities Where Love Is Grown in an Environment of Grace and in Relationships of Trust

Community Meeting

DAY SIX

In preparation for this week's meeting, you will have read and reflected upon each of the week's five Core Thoughts, recorded your thoughts and observations, and are ready to recite this week's memory verse to the group.

At This Week's Meeting

1. Open this session by asking God to help each one be aware of His gracious presence.
2. Have each member take their turn reciting to the group this week's memory verse.
3. Discuss this week's Core Thoughts, that:
   a. love grows best in community, but not all communities will grow love: bad company produces a bad environment, and bad environments reproduce more bad company, *ad infinitum ad nauseam*,
   b. healthy trees produce good fruit from which other healthy trees are grown,
   c. growing transformed relationships requires extraordinary attention and a specialized environment,

    d. transformed relationships are established within relationships of trust, and

    e. to love as Jesus loved, we must commit to our character being formed in the forge of community and grown within its safe and affirming environment of grace.

4. Allow members to briefly share any insights, questions, or illumination they have resulting from this week's daily readings and exercises.

Experience the Life

5. Play the ETL Course DVD "Week 3: Integrity."

Discussion Questions

6. As a group, discuss the ideas that Bill Hull introduced, and answer the question below.

Why can a person who wields the power of integrity accomplish great things for Christ?

Close

Share matters for the community to pray about through the following week. Pray to close the meeting.

WEEK THREE

Transformed Relationships Remain Vital Only Where Truth Is Exercised Within the Context of Love and Integrity of Character Nurtures Trust

Community Meeting

DAY SIX

In preparation for this week's meeting, you will have read and reflected upon each of the week's five Core Thoughts, recorded your thoughts and observations, and are ready to recite this week's memory verses to the group.

At This Week's Meeting

1. Open this session by asking God to help each one be aware of His gracious presence.
2. Have each member take their turn reciting to the group this week's memory verses.
3. Discuss this week's Core Thoughts, that:
   a. transformed relationships must be based upon truth and lived in the context of love,
   b. transformed relationships are built upon trust, and we will not trust and accept a message of truth until we can trust that we are truly accepted by its messenger,
   c. transformed relationships are based upon truth, and we cannot believe in the truth of the message until we can believe that the messenger is truthful,

 d. transformed relationships are the hothouses God uses to grow in us the integrity of character He will use to grow integrity of character in others, and

 e. to love as Jesus loved we must trust and accept the truth spoken in love to us by persons of integrity and develop the integrity of our character such that others can trust and accept the truth we speak to them, in love.

4. Allow members to briefly share any insights, questions, or illumination they have resulting from this week's daily readings and exercises.

Experience the Life

5. Play the ETL Course DVD "Week 4: Brokenness."

Discussion Questions

6. As a group, discuss the ideas that Bill Hull introduced, and answer the question below.

How does our lack of brokenness make it hard for us to connect with others and others to connect with us?

Close

Share matters for the community to pray about through the following week. Pray to close the meeting.

WEEK FOUR

Transformed Relationships Await Us Along the Journey of Brokenness

Community Meeting

DAY SIX

In preparation for this week's meeting, you will have read and reflected upon each of the week's five Core Thoughts, recorded your thoughts and observations, and are ready to recite this week's memory verse to the group.

At This Week's Meeting

1. Open this session by asking God to help each one be aware of His gracious presence.
2. Have each member take their turn reciting to the group this week's memory verse.
3. Discuss this week's Core Thoughts, that:
    a. the journey of brokenness is the path of everlasting life,
    b. unbrokenness is living a lie,
    c. unbrokenness is dying to die,
    d. brokenness is dying to live, and
    e. the way of brokenness leads to wholeness.
4. Allow members to briefly share any insights, questions, or illumination they have resulting from this week's daily readings and exercises.

Experience the Life

5. Play the ETL Course DVD "Week 5: Humility."

Discussion Questions

6. As a group, discuss the ideas that Bill Hull introduced, and
answer the questions below.

What is uncomplicated obedience, and why should we obey
Christ in this way?

Close

Share matters for the community to pray about through the following
week. Pray to close the meeting.

WEEK FIVE

Transformed Relationships Draw Their Strength to Sustain a Life of Living for Others from the Fertile Soil of Their Character Rich in Humility

Community Meeting

DAY SIX

In preparation for this week's meeting, you will have read and reflected upon each of the week's five Core Thoughts, recorded your thoughts and observations, and are ready to recite this week's memory verses to the group.

At This Week's Meeting

1. Open this session by asking God to help each one be aware of His gracious presence.
2. Have each member take their turn reciting to the group this week's memory verses.
3. Discuss this week's Core Thoughts, that:
   a. humility is the essential characteristic that allows God to grow His life in us,
   b. without humility, God's grace is closed off from our lives,
   c. humility is Jesus' core character trait: everything flows from it,
   d. humility flows out from us when the mind of Christ operates from within us, and
   e. to love as Jesus loved we need to enter into a life of humility, a life focused on others.
4. Allow members to briefly share any insights, questions, or

illumination they have resulting from this week's daily readings
and exercises.

Experience the Life

5. Play the ETL Course DVD "Week 6: Submission."

Discussion Questions

6. As a group, discuss the ideas that Bill Hull introduced, and
answer the question below.

How does being in an environment where others affirm our
strengths and protect our weaknesses enable us to permit others
to speak into our life?

Close

Share matters for the community to pray about through the following
week. Pray to close the meeting.

WEEK SIX

Transformed Relationships Marked by Acts of Submission Are the Evidence That One Fully Intends to Love as Jesus Loved

Community Meeting

DAY SIX

In preparation for this week's meeting, you will have read and reflected upon each of the week's five Core Thoughts, recorded your thoughts and observations, and are ready to recite this week's memory verse to the group.

At This Week's Meeting

1. Open this session by asking God to help each one be aware of His gracious presence.
2. Have each member take their turn reciting to the group this week's memory verse.
3. Discuss this week's Core Thoughts, that:
   a. the heart of Jesus' life and ministry is humility,
   b. to love as Jesus loved requires that we humbly submit ourselves in obedience to God and commit ourselves to loving others through acts service,
   c. submission should first be understood as a *love* word and only after that as an *authority* word,
   d. without submission we cannot practice humility, without humility we will not allow others to speak into our lives, and without that vulnerability, transformation won't happen, and
   e. to love as Jesus loved we must show ourselves to be in

submission to Christ by submitting to those that comprise His body, the community of Christ.

4. Allow members to briefly share any insights, questions, or illumination they have resulting from this week's daily readings and exercises.

Experience the Life

5. Play the ETL Course DVD "Book Four: Minister as Jesus Ministered," "Week 1: Called to Serve."

Discussion Questions

6. As a group, discuss the ideas that Bill Hull introduced, and answer the question below.

What does it mean to be called to the kingdom of God, to find your voice in the kingdom?

Close

Share matters for the community to pray about through the following week. Pray to close the meeting.

ABOUT THE AUTHORS

BILL HULL's mission is to call the church to return to its disciple making roots. He is a writer and discipleship evangelist calling the church to *choose the life*, a journey that Jesus called every disciple to pursue. This journey leads to a life of spiritual transformation and service. A veteran pastor, Bill has written ten books on this subject. In 1990 he founded T-NET International, a ministry devoted to transforming churches into disciple-making churches.

The core of Bill's writing is *Jesus Christ, Disciplemaker*; *The Disciple-Making Pastor*; and *The Disciple-Making Church*. He now spends his time helping leaders experience personal transformation so they can help transform their churches.

Bill and his wife, Jane, enjoy their not-so-quiet life, helping to raise their "highly energetic" grandchildren, in the beautiful Southern California sunshine.

PAUL MASCARELLA has served in local church ministry for more than twenty-five years as an associate pastor, minister of music, and worship director while holding an executive management position at a daily newspaper in Los Angeles, California. He is Associate Director of *Choose the Life Ministries*, where the abundance of his time and energy go to assisting churches as they embark on The *Choose the Life Journey*, and proceed forward with the EXPERIENCE THE LIFE series. He also serves on the board of directors for Bill Hull Ministries. He holds the bachelor of philosophy and master of theological studies degrees.

Paul and his wife, Denise, reside in Southern California.